EASY CHINESE
AND FAR EASTERN
COOKERY

EASY CHINESE
AND FAR EASTERN
COOKERY

Ho Mei Yin

Ward Lock Limited·London

© Ward Lock Limited 1982
Illustrations © Orbis-Verlag für Publizistik 1982 and
Hitgeverij Het Spectrum B.V., De Meern, Netherlands 1982

First published in Great Britain in 1982
by Ward Lock Limited, 82 Gower Street,
London WC1E 6EQ, a Pentos Company.

Text filmset in Sabon
by MS Filmsetting Limited, Frome, Somerset

Printed and bound in Hong Kong by
Lee Fung Asco Ltd

British Library Cataloguing in Publication Data

Easy Chinese and Far Eastern cookery.
   1. Cookery, Chinese   2. Cookery, Oriental
641.5951   TX724.5.C5

ISBN 0–7063–6205–5

Notes

It is important to follow *either* the metric *or* the Imperial measures when using the recipes in this book.

All spoon measures are level.

Each dish will serve four people, unless indicated otherwise.

Flour is plain and sugar is granulated, unless indicated otherwise.

Unusual ingredients may be purchased from Chinese supermarkets and other oriental food shops.

CONTENTS

SOUPS

Basic Chinese Chicken Stock

1·5 kg/3 lb boiling chicken, quartered
2 litres/3½ pints water
1 small onion, chopped
3 sticks celery, chopped
1 small piece root ginger, crushed
1 tablespoon dry sherry
1 teaspoon salt

Place the chicken pieces in a large, heavy saucepan. Add the water and bring to the boil. Skim off any froth or bits which rise to the surface. Reduce the heat and simmer, covered, for 1½ hours.

Remove the chicken pieces from the pan and discard; all their flavour will have cooked out. Add the onion, celery and ginger to the stock and allow to stand for 20 minutes. Then add the sherry and salt and simmer for 10 minutes. Strain the stock through a clean cloth and leave to cool completely. Then skim off the fat which will have risen to the surface.

Basic Chinese Meat Stock

450 g/1 lb lean pork
250 g/9 oz chicken wings, carcass, giblets, etc.
2 litres/3½ pints water
2 carrots, chopped
1 small onion, chopped
1 piece root ginger, crushed
1 teaspoon salt
2 teaspoons soy sauce

Place the pork and chicken in a large, heavy saucepan. Add the water and bring slowly to the boil. Skim off any froth or bits which rise to the surface. Reduce the heat and simmer, covered, for 20 minutes. Remove the pork and chicken from the pan; they can be kept for other dishes. Add the carrots, onion and ginger to the stock and simmer for 30 minutes. Add the salt and soy sauce and simmer for a further 5 minutes. Strain the stock through a clean cloth and leave to cool completely. Then skim off the fat which will have risen to the surface.

Chinese Pork and Bean Sprout Soup

20 g/¾ oz dried Chinese mushrooms
50 g/2 oz transparent noodles
300 g/10 oz lean pork
4 tablespoons oil
1 onion, chopped
1 clove garlic, chopped
150 g/5 oz canned bean sprouts, drained
1·5 litres/2½ pints hot chicken stock
salt, pepper
2 tablespoons soy sauce
sugar

Soak the mushrooms in warm water for 15 to 30 minutes, until swollen. Cut the noodles into 10 cm/4 inch lengths. Put them into a bowl and cover with boiling salted water. Allow to stand for 5 minutes. Drain, rinse with cold water and drain again. Drain the mushrooms, and halve or quarter them if large. While the mushrooms and noodles are soaking, cut the pork into narrow strips.

Heat the oil in a pan and fry the pork on all sides for 5 minutes. Remove and keep hot. Fry the onion and garlic in the pan for 3 minutes, until just soft. Put the pork back in the pan, and add the bean sprouts, noodles, mushrooms and stock. Season with salt, pepper, the soy sauce and a pinch sugar. Bring to the boil and simmer for 8 minutes. Serve in warmed soup bowls.

Wonton Soup

Hun-t'un-t'ang

SERVES 6

100 g/4 oz flour
salt
1 egg
1 tablespoon milk
2 tablespoons oil
100 g/4 oz spinach, washed and
  picked over

100 g/4 oz minced pork
2 teaspoons soy sauce
ground ginger
1.5 litres/2½ pints chicken stock
  (see page 8)
1 tablespoon chopped chives

Wontons are small, stuffed pastry parcels; they are usually
eaten as an accompaniment to soup.

   To make the wontons, sieve the flour and a pinch of salt
into a bowl. Break in the egg and add the milk and oil. Mix to
a firm but pliant dough. Roll out very thinly on a lightly
floured surface. Cut into 7.5 cm/3 inch squares. Cover with a
cloth while preparing the stuffing.

   To make the stuffing, put the spinach into a bowl, pour
boiling water over and leave for 3 minutes. Drain well and
chop. Put the pork in a bowl and stir in the soy sauce and a
pinch ground ginger. Add the spinach and mix.

   Put 1 teaspoon of stuffing in the centre of each pastry
square. Fold over one side of the pastry to form a roll,
pressing to seal the long edge. Fold the two ends of pastry at
the ends of the roll over each other and press together. Bring
the stock to the boil in a large saucepan. Add the wontons
and simmer, covered, for 20 minutes. Divide the wontons into
soup bowls and pour the stock over them. Sprinkle with
chives and serve.

Chinese Asparagus Soup

Hay Hong Lo Soen

900 ml/1½ pints chicken stock
  (see page 6)
150 g/5 oz leeks, sliced
1 clove garlic
salt, pepper, ground ginger,
  curry powder

1 tablespoon dripping
2 tablespoons soy sauce
175 g/6 oz canned crabmeat,
  drained
250 g/9 oz canned asparagus
  spears, drained

Bring the chicken stock to the boil in a large saucepan, add
the leeks and simmer for 20 minutes. Crush the garlic with
salt. Melt the dripping in another pan and fry the garlic until
golden. Add to the soup. Then add the soy sauce and
seasonings to taste. Remove any hard pieces from the
crabmeat, flake it and add to the soup. Add the asparagus
spears, then heat them in the soup. Adjust seasoning and
serve.

Chinese Noodle Soup

SERVES 6

200 g/7 oz boned leg of pork
2 tablespoons Chinese rice wine
  or dry sherry
2 tablespoons soy sauce
salt, pepper, ground ginger
10 g/⅓ oz dried Chinese
  mushrooms
150 g/5 oz canned bamboo
  shoots, drained

100 g/4 oz canned chicken,
  drained
100 g/4 oz cooked ham, sliced
250 g/9 oz Chinese noodles
2 litres/3½ pints chicken stock
  (see page 6)
oil for frying
sprigs cress

Cut the pork into small strips. Mix the rice wine or sherry,
soy sauce and seasonings to taste in a bowl. Add the pork,
cover and leave to marinate for 1 hour. After 30 minutes put
the mushrooms to soak in warm water for 15 to 30 minutes,
until swollen. Meanwhile prepare the other ingredients. Cut
the bamboo shoots into thin strips and cut the chicken into
2.5 cm/1 inch cubes. Trim any fat from the ham and cut into
2.5 cm/1 inch squares. Bring a pan of salted water to the boil.
Add the noodles and simmer for 10 minutes. Drain in a sieve,
rinse in cold water and drain again. Drain the mushrooms.

   Put the stock, mushrooms, bamboo shoots and noodles
into a large saucepan. Heat gently for 3 minutes. Meanwhile
take the pork out of the marinade and drain. Heat the oil in a
frying pan and fry the pork strips on all sides for 2 minutes.
Remove and add to the soup with the chicken and ham
pieces. Heat through gently. Pour the soup into warmed soup
bowls, sprinkle with cress and serve.

Chinese noodle soup

Chinese Vegetable Soup

250 g/9 oz lean pork
5 tablespoons soy sauce
2 teaspoons flour
salt, pepper, ground ginger
2 carrots
100 g/4 oz canned bamboo
  shoots, drained
50 g/2 oz spinach, washed and
  picked over

2 tablespoons oil
1·5 litres/2½ pints hot stock
50 g/2 oz fresh mushrooms,
  thinly sliced
15 g/½ oz transparent noodles
2 tablespoons Chinese rice wine
  or dry sherry

Cut the pork into narrow strips. Mix 2 tablespoons soy sauce
with the flour in a cup. Season to taste with salt and pepper.
Put the meat in a bowl, spoon the marinade over it, cover and
leave to stand for 10 minutes. Meanwhile cut the carrots and
bamboo shoots into thin strips. Cut the spinach leaves
through once.

Heat the oil in a large saucepan. Remove the meat from the
marinade, drain and fry in the oil, on all sides, for 10 minutes.
Add the stock to the pan with the carrots and simmer for
another 10 minutes. Add the bamboo shoots, mushrooms and
noodles and simmer for a further 10 minutes, until just
tender. Five minutes before the end of the cooking time add
the spinach leaves. Season to taste with the remaining soy
sauce, the rice wine or sherry, ginger and salt. Serve at once in
warmed soup bowls.

Kiemblo

Chinese soup with vegetables, minced beef and dumplings

1 slice wholemeal bread, crusts
  removed
250 g/9 oz minced beef
salt, pepper
1·5 litres/2½ pints stock
1 tablespoon oil
1 onion, sliced
150 g/5 oz savoy cabbage,
  chopped

1 leek, sliced
50 g/2 oz fresh mushrooms,
  sliced
175 g/6 oz celery, sliced
50 g/2 oz frozen peas
100 g/4 oz ribbon noodles
1 tablespoon soy sauce
3 tablespoons Chinese rice wine
  or dry sherry

Soak the bread in a little water and squeeze out the excess.
Mix the beef and bread together and season to taste. Shape
into small oval dumplings with a teaspoon. Bring the stock to
the boil in a pan, put in the dumplings, and simmer for 10
minutes. Meanwhile heat the oil in a large saucepan, add the
onion, and fry for 3 minutes until pale brown. Add the
cabbage, leek, mushrooms and celery and fry for another 5
minutes. Take the dumplings out of the stock, drain and keep
warm. Strain the stock on to the vegetable mixture. Add the
peas and noodles and simmer for 15 minutes, until the peas
and noodles are done. Put the dumplings back into the soup,
add the soy sauce and rice wine or sherry, and season to taste.
Serve at once.

Kiemblo

Peking Hot-sour Soup

10 g/⅓ oz dried Chinese
 mushrooms
100 g/4 oz lean pork
1 piece bamboo (fresh or
 canned)
½ cake bean curd
1 egg
water to mix
1 tablespoon cornflour

1 litre/1¾ pints chicken stock (see
 (see page 6)
2 tablespoons white vinegar
1½ tablespoons soy sauce
salt, pepper
½ teaspoon sesame oil
1 tablespoon chopped chives
 or 1 spring onion, chopped
 (optional)

Soak the mushrooms in warm water for 15 to 30 minutes,
until swollen. Drain, remove the stalks, and cut the caps into
thin strips. Cut the pork and bamboo into thin strips, and the
bean curd into slightly thicker strips. Beat the egg in a bowl
with 1 teaspoon water. Mix the cornflour to a smooth paste
with 4 tablespoons water.

 Bring the stock to the boil in a large saucepan, add the
meat and mushrooms, and simmer for 8 minutes. Add the
bamboo and bean curd and simmer for a further 4 minutes.
Stir in the vinegar and soy sauce and season to taste. Bring to
the boil and stir in the egg. When the egg has set in swirls, stir
in the cornflour paste until the soup binds and becomes clear
and glossy. Then stir in the oil. Serve in warmed soup bowls
and sprinkle with chopped chives or spring onion if desired.

Vietnamese Abalone Soup

1 litre/1¾ pints good clear stock
90 g/3½ oz long-grain rice
175 g/6 oz canned abalone
2 tablespoons oil

1 onion, chopped
1 clove garlic, crushed
salt, pepper, allspice
1 sprig tarragon, chopped

If you have no good stock available use canned consommé or
a stock cube for this recipe. Bring the stock to the boil in a
large saucepan. Add the rice and boil for 15 minutes, until
tender. Meanwhile drain the abalone, reserving the liquid,
and cut the shellfish into strips. Heat the oil in a frying pan,
add the onion, and fry until lightly browned. Add the abalone
and garlic, and stew gently for a few minutes. Then add to
the rice-stock mixture with the reserved abalone liquid.
Reheat and add the seasonings to taste. Serve the soup in
warmed soup bowls and sprinkle the tarragon over the top.

Indonesian Chicken Soup

Soto ajam

salt, pepper
2 litres/3½ pints water
1·5 kg/3 lb boiling chicken
1 small onion, sliced
5 cloves garlic, sliced
1 tablespoon ground ginger
200 g/7 oz canned bean sprouts,
 drained

250 g/9 oz canned celery, drained
 and chopped
100 ml/4 fl oz sherry
soy sauce
4 hard-boiled eggs, chopped
1 tablespoon chopped chives

Add salt to the water and bring to the boil in a large pan. Put
in the chicken, cover and simmer for 1 hour, or until tender.

 Remove the chicken from the stock and put aside. Then
add to the stock the onion, garlic, ginger, and pepper to taste.
Simmer for 15 minutes. Meanwhile remove the skin from the
chicken, take the meat off the bones and cut into small, even-
sized pieces. Keep warm. Mix the bean sprouts and celery in a
bowl with the sherry. Season to taste with soy sauce. Put the
chicken pieces into a warmed soup tureen, add the vegetables
and eggs, and pour the stock on top. Sprinkle with chives and
serve.

Indonesian chicken soup

STARTERS, SAUCES AND SIDE DISHES

Spring Rolls

250 g/9 oz flour
350 ml/12 fl oz water
1½ teaspoons groundnut oil
salt, cayenne
4 tablespoons oil
125 g/4½ oz minced pork
125 g/4½ oz minced beef
250 g/9 oz white cabbage or
  Chinese cabbage, cut into thin
  strips
1 leek, cut into thin strips
1 onion, finely chopped

225 g/8 oz canned bamboo
  shoots, drained and cut into
  thin strips
100 g/4 oz canned mushrooms,
  drained and chopped
200 g/7 oz canned bean sprouts,
  drained
4 tablespoons soy sauce
4 tablespoons Chinese rice wine
  or dry sherry
groundnut oil for frying
1 egg yolk, beaten
oil for deep frying

First make the batter. Place the flour in a bowl and gradually stir in the water, stirring in the same direction all the time. Stir in the 1½ teaspoons groundnut oil and a pinch salt. Cover and leave to stand for 30 minutes.

To prepare the stuffing, heat the 4 tablespoons oil in a pan. Add the minced meats and fry for 2 minutes, stirring. Add the strips of cabbage and leek, the onion and the bamboo shoots, and fry gently for 5 minutes. Add the mushrooms and bean sprouts, and stew for a further 2 minutes. Season with the soy sauce, rice wine or sherry, salt and cayenne. Set aside.

Lightly paint the surface of a large frying pan with groundnut oil. Pour in an eighth of the batter, spread it out evenly by tilting the pan, and cook over a very gentle heat until firm and lightly browned on both sides. Make 7 other pancakes in the same way, placing them between damp tea towels when cooked.

Cut the 8 pancakes into 8 large squares. Divide the stuffing between the pancakes, spreading it out on the surface. Fold two opposite corners towards the middle. Starting with one of the other corners (the one nearest to you) roll up the pancake. Paint the last corner with beaten egg yolk and press the roll well together. Heat the oil to a temperature of 180°C/350°F and deep fry the spring rolls. Take them out, drain on absorbent paper and serve on a warmed dish.

Sweet-and-sour Sauce

20 g/¾ oz cornflour
100 ml/4 fl oz water
40 g/1½ oz soft brown sugar
150 ml/¼ pint red wine
3 tablespoons tomato ketchup
1 tablespoon soy sauce
1 teaspoon mustard powder

1 green pepper, seeded and
  finely chopped
1 large, firm tomato, skinned,
  seeded and finely chopped
3 slices canned pineapple,
  drained and finely chopped
salt, pepper

Mix together the cornflour and water in a pan until smooth. Add the sugar, wine, tomato ketchup, soy sauce and mustard powder. Bring slowly to the boil, stirring continuously. Boil for 2 minutes, until the sauce turns clear. Then add the pepper, tomato and pineapple. Bring the sauce back to the boil and adjust seasoning to taste. Serve in a warmed sauceboat.

Peacock Platter

The peacock platter is a cold Chinese hors d'oeuvre consisting of thinly sliced meats and other ingredients, and it is served on special occasions. If prepared and arranged with care, the dish looks like the outspread tail of a displaying peacock. It is impossible to give an exact recipe: it can be as simple or as elaborate as you like. Among possible ingredients are: boiled or steamed chicken, red-cooked meat or poultry, ham and abalone. All ingredients are very thinly sliced and then arranged in the form of a fan on a flat dish.

As can be seen from the picture, slices of hard-boiled eggs, decorated with red and green cocktail cherries, can be used to represent the eyes of the peacock. Other decoration can be provided by figures cut out of carrots or radishes. Asparagus, cucumber slices, radish roses, pieces of pineapple, and anything else you like can be used to decorate the peacock's tail. Hoisin and plum sauce can be served as dips, and can be bought ready-prepared from oriental food shops.

Peacock platter

Sambal Goreng Hati

Liver sambal

250–300 g/9–10 oz calves' liver
1 small onion, chopped
1 clove garlic, crushed
1½ teaspoons chilli sauce
1 teaspoon galingale (optional)
1 teaspoon soft brown sugar
½ teaspoon belacan (prawn paste)

1 teaspoon salt
3 tablespoons oil
1 tablespoon tamarind pulp, chopped
225 ml/7 fl oz coconut milk

Soak the liver in cold water for 15 minutes. Remove from the water, pat dry with absorbent paper, and cut into short, thin strips. Pound and mash together the onion, garlic, chilli sauce, galingale, sugar, belacan (prawn paste) and salt. Heat the oil in a heavy-based pan and fry the mixture. Add the liver and continue frying over medium heat, turning occasionally, until the liver starts to brown. Add the tamarind and stir for 1 minute. Pour in the coconut milk and allow to simmer for 5 minutes, or until the liver is done. Serve as a side dish with a Malaysian or Indonesian-style meal.

Sambal Goreng Telur

Egg Sambal

3 red chilli peppers, chopped
4 red onions, chopped
2 cloves garlic, crushed
½ teaspoon belacan (prawn paste)
2 teaspoons galingale (optional)
2½ teaspoons soft brown sugar

1 tablespoon tamarind pulp, chopped
salt
2 tablespoons oil
250 ml/8 fl oz coconut milk
2 bay leaves
4 hard-boiled eggs

Pound and mash together the chillies, onions, garlic, belacan (prawn paste), galingale, brown sugar and tamarind. Season to taste with salt. Heat the oil in a heavy-based pan, add the mashed ingredients and fry gently for 2 to 3 minutes. Add the coconut milk and bay leaves, stir, and simmer for a few minutes. Add the eggs and simmer gently, stirring occasionally, until the oil separates from the sauce. Remove the eggs from the pan, let them cool a little, and halve them lengthways. Place them on a dish with the rounded side uppermost. Pour the sauce over and serve immediately as a hot side dish with a Malaysian or Indonesian-style dinner.

Sambal Taoco

Soy-bean hot sauce

8–10 red chilli peppers, seeded and finely chopped
3–4 red onions, chopped
  or 1 large onion, chopped
3 cloves garlic, crushed
½ teaspoon belacan (prawn paste)

1 teaspoon galingale (optional)
1 teaspoon soft brown sugar
2–3 tablespoons oil
3–4 tablespoons soy-bean paste
1 tablespoon tamarind pulp, chopped
3–4 tablespoons water

Thoroughly pound and mash together the chillies, onions, garlic, belacan (prawn paste), galingale and sugar. Heat the oil in a heavy-based pan, add the spice mixture and fry for 2 to 3 minutes. Add the soy-bean paste, tamarind and water and simmer gently until all the oil has been absorbed. Let the sambal cool to room temperature, and then transfer to a clean glass jar. Store the sambal, with the jar tightly stoppered, in the refrigerator.

Sambal Bajak

Hot sauce

8–10 red chilli peppers, seeded and finely chopped
4–6 red onions, chopped
  or 2–3 small onions, chopped
2 cloves garlic, crushed
8 blanched almonds, crushed
1 teaspoon belacan (prawn paste)

1 tablespoon soft brown sugar
1 teaspoon salt
2 tablespoons oil
2 tablespoons tamarind pulp, chopped
1 bay leaf
2 tablespoons water

Thoroughly pound and mash together the chillies, onions, garlic, nuts, belacan (prawn paste), sugar and salt. Heat the oil in a heavy-based pan and fry the spice mixture in it for 2 to 3 minutes. Add the tamarind, bay leaf and water, and continue simmering over medium heat until all the oil has been absorbed. Stir continuously to prevent sticking, especially as the ingredients become drier. Remove the bay leaf, let the sambal cool to room temperature, and then transfer to a clean glass jar. Store the sambal, with the jar tightly stoppered, in the refrigerator.

Rempeyek ikan terie

Siu Pai Quat

Spare ribs

1 kg/2 lb spare ribs of pork	3 tablespoons soy sauce
1 teaspoon salt	1 tablespoon sake, Chinese rice
1 teaspoon sugar	wine or dry sherry
1 clove garlic, crushed	2 tablespoons hoisin sauce
1 teaspoon chopped root ginger	2 tablespoons honey

The spare ribs needed for this recipe have to be specially
asked for from the butcher; they are the very short ribs,
10–14cm/4–5½ inches long, with not much meat on them,
from near the blade bone of the pig. The butcher will cut a
row of them – joined together, not separated into chops. Cut
down through the meat, about halfway between the chops.

Rub the ribs with the salt and sugar and leave for 1 hour.
Pound and mash together the garlic and ginger, and mix with
the soy sauce, sake (or rice wine or sherry), hoisin sauce and
honey. Marinate the meat in this mixture for 3 hours, turning
regularly.

Drain the ribs, reserving the marinade. Place the ribs on a
rack in a roasting pan containing water, and bake for 1 hour
at 170–190°C/325–375°F/gas 3–4. Then turn the oven up to
maximum heat and bake the ribs for a further 5 to 10
minutes. Remove from the oven, separate the ribs with a
knife and serve as an hors d'oeuvre to a Chinese meal,
accompanied by spring onion tassels (see page 77).

Rempeyek Ikan Teri

Dried fish pancakes

25 g/1 oz dried ikan teri	3 blanched almonds, mashed
or 25 g/1 oz canned anchovies	salt
2 cloves garlic, crushed	3–5 tablespoons coconut milk
½ teaspoon ground coriander	100 g/4 oz rice flour
½ teaspoon turmeric	oil for frying

Ikan teri are tiny, anchovy-like dried fish that can be eaten
whole, although some people prefer to snap the heads off
first. These dried fish are sold in oriental food shops,
sometimes curried. When the fish are to be fried, as in this
recipe, it is advisable to dry them out a little more, either in
the sun, or indoors near the fire or a radiator. (Canned
anchovies will, of course, need drying completely.)

Pound and mash together the garlic, coriander, turmeric,
nuts and a pinch salt. Stir sufficient coconut milk into the
flour to make a smooth batter, not too thin. Stir the fish and
the spice mixture into the batter, and leave to stand for 10
minutes. Heat a film of oil in a wok or frying pan. Stir the
batter again, put a spoonful into the pan and tip so that it
quickly spreads to cover the base of the pan. Fry to a golden
brown on both sides, remove from the pan and drain on
absorbent paper. Keep warm. Continue until all the batter
has been cooked. Serve as a side dish with a Malaysian or
Indonesian-style meal.

FISH AND SHELLFISH

Japanese Fish in Sweet-and-sour Sauce

Uwo no Amazukake

600 g/1¼ lb fillets of white fish	150 ml/¼ pint water
juice ½ lemon	25 g/1 oz sugar
5 tablespoons soy sauce	3 slices lemon
salt	oil for deep frying
25 g/1 oz potato flour	25 g/1 oz cornflour
5 tablespoons vinegar	

Wash the fish fillets under the cold tap and pat dry with absorbent paper. Put them in a bowl and trickle the lemon juice over. Add 2 tablespoons soy sauce. Turn the fish in the marinade, then cut into strips 3 cm/1¼ inches wide. Leave to marinate for 15 minutes. Season with salt and toss in the potato flour. Form the strips of fish into sausage shapes with your hands.

To make the sauce, put the vinegar, water, sugar, remaining soy sauce and the lemon slices in a pan. Bring to the boil, then reduce the heat and simmer very gently for 20 minutes. Meanwhile, deep fry the fish in the oil for about 8 minutes. Remove from the oil, drain on absorbent paper and keep warm. Finally, thicken the sauce. Mix the cornflour to a smooth paste in a cup with a little cold water. Blend a little of the hot sauce into the mixture, then return to the pan. Bring slowly to the boil, stirring constantly. Simmer for 2 to 3 minutes to allow the flour to cook through.

To serve, arrange the fish on a warmed dish. The sauce can either be poured over, or served separately in a jug.

Chinese Fish

Ten Tjiun yu

1 trout (400 g/14 oz), cleaned	3 tablespoons soy sauce
1 carp (1.5 kg/3 lb), cleaned and scaled	300 ml/½ pint hot water
juice 1¼ lemons	4 large savoy cabbage leaves
salt, pepper, ground star anise	2 teaspoons cornflour
50 g/2 oz smoked ham	40 g/1½ oz pork dripping
450 g/1 lb fresh mushrooms, sliced	1 tablespoon chopped parsley
2 pieces preserved stem ginger, sliced	1 lemon, cut into slices

Wash both fish under the cold tap and pat dry with absorbent paper. Season inside and out with the juice 1 lemon. Make several cuts across the backs of both fish. Rub in salt and pepper. Cut the ham into thin strips and insert into the cuts. Grease an oval ovenproof dish and put the fish in it. Mix together the mushrooms and ginger and scatter over the fish. Pour the soy sauce over and sprinkle with a pinch ground star anise. Add a little of the hot water, cover and place in the oven. Bake for 30 minutes at 200°C/400°F/gas 6.

While the fish is baking add the rest of the hot water gradually. Baste the fish from time to time with the cooking liquid. Remove when cooked and arrange on the cabbage leaves in a warmed dish. Keep warm.

Stir the fish juices from the baking dish with a little cold water and bring to the boil. To thicken the sauce, mix the cornflour to a smooth paste in a cup with a little cold water. Blend a little of the hot liquid into the mixture, then return to the baking dish. Bring slowly to the boil, stirring constantly. Simmer for 2 to 3 minutes to allow the flour to cook through. Pour into a sauce boat to serve separately and keep warm. Finally heat the dripping in a small pan. Pour over the fish with the juice ½ lemon. Garnish with the parsley and lemon slices and serve with the sauce.

Oriental Fish with Grapefruit

750 g/1½ lb fillet of cod
1 grapefruit, halved
25 g/1 oz butter
1 small onion, chopped
25 g/1 oz flour
300 ml/½ pint double cream
salt, pepper, ground ginger
2 hard-boiled eggs,
 chopped

COURT BOUILLON
1 onion
1 bay leaf
4 cloves
1 litre/1¾ pints water
3 tablespoons white wine
 vinegar
1 teaspoon salt
4 peppercorns

Divide the cod fillet into four portions. Wash the fish under the cold tap and pat dry with absorbent paper. To make the court bouillon, peel the onion and make several deep cuts in it. Insert the bay leaf and cloves into the cuts. Bring the water, vinegar and salt to the boil in a large pan, then add the onion and peppercorns. Add the fish to the pan and poach gently for 15 minutes, until done. Meanwhile squeeze the juice from one grapefruit half. Divide the other half into segments, remove pith and skin, chop coarsely and set aside. Remove the fish from the court bouillon and keep warm. Reserve 300 ml/½ pint of the liquid.

Melt the butter in a pan. Fry the onion for 5 minutes, until golden. Scatter in the flour and simmer for 3 minutes, stirring. Add the reserved court bouillon and bring to the boil, still stirring. Simmer for 8 minutes. Stir in the cream and grapefruit juice. Put the sauce through a strainer. Season to taste with salt, pepper and a pinch ground ginger. Arrange the fish on a warmed serving dish, pour the sauce over, and garnish with the eggs and grapefuit pieces. Serve at once.

Oriental fish with grapefruit

Steamed Bream

1 bream or other firm-fleshed
  sea fish, cleaned and scaled
1 teaspoon salt
2 teaspoons oil
1 leek
1 small piece root ginger, peeled
  and finely chopped
1½ tablespoons sake, Chinese
  rice wine or dry sherry
1 tablespoon soy sauce
½ teaspoon sugar
8 spring onion tassels (see
  page 77)

Do not remove the head and tail when cleaning the fish. Wash
the cleaned fish under the cold tap and pat dry with absorbent
paper. Make a few, shallow, diagonal cuts on either side of
the fish. Rub in the salt and then the oil. Place the fish on its
side in a flameproof serving dish just large enough for it. Cut
the leek into 5 cm/2 inch strips. Cover the fish with the leek
and the chopped ginger. Mix the sake (or rice wine, or
sherry), soy sauce and sugar, and stir until the sugar has
dissolved. Pour this sauce over the fish and place the dish in a
large steamer. Steam for 30 to 40 minutes. Remove the dish
from the steamer, arrange the spring onion tassels around the
fish, and serve at once.

Kyoto Fish Fillets

1 kg/2 lb fillets of firm white fish
100 ml/4 fl oz sake
100 ml/4 fl oz oil
3 tablespoons sweet rice wine
  or sweet sherry
6 egg yolks, beaten
salt
sugar

Rinse the fish under cold water, pat dry with absorbent paper,
and cut into cubes. Place the cubes in a bowl, pour the sake
over them, cover the bowl and allow to stand for 30 minutes.
Take out the fish, drain and pat dry. Heat the oil in a large
frying pan. Add the fish and fry on all sides for 10 minutes,
until just cooked.

Beat the sweet rice wine or sherry into the egg yolks, and
season generously with salt and sugar. Pour this mixture over
the fish, and cook gently for 3 minutes to allow the egg
mixture to thicken. Transfer to a warmed dish and serve at
once.

Kyoto fish fillets

Oriental fish kebabs

Oriental Fish Kebabs

1 kg/2 lb fillets of red mullet
4 small onions, halved
8 small tomatoes, halved
4 tablespoons olive oil
2 tablespoons sherry
1 teaspoon sugar
salt, pepper

MARINADE
1 clove garlic
salt
juice 2 lemons

SAUCE
200 g/7 oz yogurt
150 ml/¼ pint soured cream
1 teaspoon chopped parsley
1 teaspoon chopped chives
salt

These fish kebabs taste best grilled over charcoal, but an ordinary gas or electric grill will still produce good results. Wash the mullet fillets under the cold tap and pat dry with absorbent paper. Cut into slices 1 cm/½ inch thick, across the grain of the flesh. To make the marinade: crush the garlic with salt and mix in a bowl with the lemon juice. Add the fish slices and marinate for 15 minutes, turning frequently.

Meanwhile bring a pan of water to the boil and briefly blanch the onion halves. Drain the fish slices and roll them up. Place alternate rolls of fish, tomato and onion on skewers. Mix the oil, sherry, sugar, and salt and pepper to taste with 2 tablespoons of the marinade. Brush the kebabs with this mixture. Put them on a rack under the grill, with the grill pan below to catch the drips. Grill for 10 minutes, turning frequently, and brushing with the oil, sherry and marinade mixture.

While the kebabs are grilling, prepare the sauce. Beat the yogurt and cream together in a bowl until foamy. Add the parsley and chives and season with salt. Serve the kebabs and sauce separately.

Singapore Fish with Curry Sauce

4 halibut steaks (250g/9oz each)
juice 1½ lemons
100 ml/4 fl oz stock
100 ml/4 fl oz white wine
1 bay leaf
salt, pepper
75 g/3 oz butter
30 g/1¼ oz curry powder
30 g/1¼ oz flour
150 ml/¼ pint water
40 g/1½ oz apple purée
1 teaspoon sugar
225 g/8 oz canned button
 mushrooms, drained
1 banana

Pat the halibut steaks dry with absorbent paper and sprinkle them with the juice of 1 lemon. Bring the stock and wine to the boil in a large saucepan. Add the bay leaf and salt, and carefully put the fish into the pan. Poach for 10 minutes, until just cooked. Remove the fish from the pan, drain, and arrange on a warmed serving dish. Keep hot. Strain and reserve the fish stock in the pan.

To make the curry sauce, melt 40 g/1½ oz of the butter in a pan, add the curry powder and flour, and cook gently for 3 minutes. Pour the reserved fish stock and the water into the pan, stirring. Bring to the boil and simmer for 5 minutes. Then stir in the apple purée, and season the sauce with the remaining lemon juice, salt, pepper and the sugar. Reheat gently without boiling.

Melt 25 g/1 oz of the butter in a frying pan, and fry the mushrooms for 5 minutes. Season with salt and pepper, remove and keep hot. Peel the banana, cut it in half widthways, then cut each piece in half lengthways. Melt the remaining butter in another frying pan and fry the banana pieces for 2 minutes each side, until golden. To serve, arrange the mushrooms on top of the halibut steaks, garnish with the banana pieces, and pour the sauce around the fish.

Right: South Seas fish

Below: Malaysian fish curry

Malaysian Fish Curry

850 g/1¾ lb fillets of firm
  white fish
2 tablespoons lemon juice
salt, ground ginger
25 g/1 oz curry powder
flour for coating

4 tablespoons groundnut oil
butter for frying
3 onions, sliced
4 tablespoons milk
50 g/2 oz peanuts, halved
150 ml/¼ pint double cream

Wash the fish under the cold tap and pat dry with absorbent
paper. Cut into 4 cm/1½ inch cubes and place on a dish.
Trickle the lemon juice over the fish, cover and allow to stand
for 10 minutes.

Sprinkle salt and half the curry powder over the fish and
coat with flour. Heat the oil in a large pan and fry the fish
cubes on all sides for 3 minutes, until light brown. Transfer to
a serving dish and keep warm. Melt the butter in another pan.
Dip the onion rings in milk, then in flour, and fry in the hot
fat for 5 minutes, until golden brown. Remove, drain and
place over the fish cubes. Add the peanuts to the groundnut
oil in which the fish was cooked with a pinch each salt and
ground ginger, the cream and remaining curry powder.
Simmer gently for 2 minutes over low heat. Pour over the fish
and serve.

South Seas Fish

SERVES 5

5 cod steaks (200 g/7 oz each)
150 ml/¼ pint lemon juice
salt, pepper, ground mace,
  powdered saffron
40 g/1½ oz butter
2 onions, chopped
600 ml/1 pint water

1 teaspoon ginger syrup (from
  jar preserved stem ginger)
grated rind 2 lemons
30 g/1¼ oz flour
4 eggs, beaten
1 teaspoon chopped parsley

Rinse the fish under cold water and pat dry with absorbent
paper. Sprinkle with 1½ tablespoons lemon juice and allow to
stand for 10 minutes. Season the fish with salt and pepper.
Melt the butter in a large pan and fry the onions until soft.
Then add the fish steaks and brown on all sides for 5 minutes.
Add the water, ginger syrup, lemon rind, remaining lemon
juice and a pinch mace, and bring to the boil. Simmer over
low heat for 10 minutes.

Meanwhile, stir the flour into the eggs, and season with
saffron. Add a little of the liquid from the fish, and season
with more salt if necessary. Stir in the parsley. Pour the
mixture over the fish. Stirring carefully, bring the contents of
the pan to just below boiling point. Take the pan off the heat,
arrange the fish in a serving dish, pour on the sauce, and serve
at once.

Fish in soy sauce

Fish in Soy Sauce

1 haddock, cod or mullet
(850 g/1¾ lb), cleaned
juice 1 lemon
225 g/8 oz pork fillet, thinly
sliced
flour for coating
1 leek
80 ml/3 fl oz oil
1 piece preserved stem ginger,
sliced
100 g/4 oz canned bamboo
shoots, drained and sliced
150 g/5 oz canned mushrooms,
drained

FISH MARINADE
1 tablespoon soy sauce

1 tablespoon Chinese rice wine
or dry sherry
salt, pepper, ground ginger

MEAT MARINADE
1 tablespoon soy sauce
1 tablespoon Chinese rice wine
or dry sherry
1 teaspoon flour

SAUCE
2 tablespoons Chinese rice wine
or dry sherry
2 tablespoons soy sauce
sugar
salt
150 ml/¼ pint stock

Cut the head off the fish. Wash the fish under the cold tap and
pat dry with absorbent paper. Trickle the lemon juice over it
and leave to stand. Mix the ingredients for the fish marinade
in a jug. Slash the fish several times across the backbone, put
in a dish, pour over the marinade and leave to stand for 30
minutes. Meanwhile coat the pork slices in flour. Mix the
ingredients for the meat marinade in a bowl, add the pork
and turn from time to time. To make the sauce: mix the rice
wine or sherry, soy sauce and a pinch each sugar and salt in a
bowl. Add the stock and keep aside. Then cut the leek into
strips.

Remove the fish and pork from their marinades and drain.
Heat the oil in a pan large enough to take the fish. Add the
ginger and leek and fry, stirring, for 5 minutes. Remove from
the pan and keep warm. Put the fish in the pan and brown on
both sides (2 minutes each side). Add the bamboo shoots,
pork and mushrooms, and return the leek and ginger to the
pan. Pour the sauce over the fish and vegetables. Cover the
pan and bring the contents to boiling point. Then reduce the
heat and simmer for 15 minutes, until the fish is done.
Transfer to a warmed dish and serve.

Japanese Salad

Sarada Modan

SERVES 6
salt, paprika
1 cucumber, grated
2 carrots, grated
1 large white Japanese radish,
grated
100 g/4 oz fresh mushrooms,
sliced
325 g/11 oz crawfish tails, halved
1 tablespoon chopped parsley
1 tablespoon chopped borage
1 tablespoon chopped dill

2 eggs
sugar
50 g/2 oz butter, melted
2 tablespoons white wine
vinegar
1 peach, sliced
1 mandarin orange, divided into
segments, pith and skin
removed
½ orange, sliced

Sprinkle salt over the grated vegetables and leave for 30
minutes; pour off the liquid that will have been drawn. Then
mix the vegetables with the mushrooms. Add the crawfish
tails and herbs. Mix and leave to stand for 15 minutes.
Meanwhile make the dressing. Whisk together the eggs, a
pinch each salt and sugar, and the butter in a heatproof bowl
over a pan of hot water until foamy. Remove the bowl from
the heat and gradually stir in the vinegar. Continue stirring
until the sauce is cold. Season to taste with paprika. Arrange
the grated vegetable mixture in a bowl and pour the sauce
over the salad. Garnish with the peach, mandarin and orange
slices.

Crab with Sherry

75 g/3 oz canned crabmeat
5 eggs
salt, pepper
2 teaspoons dry sherry
3 tablespoons oil
2 spring onions *or* 1 small onion,
finely chopped

50 g/2 oz fresh mushrooms,
sliced
1 tablespoon chopped chives or
parsley

Drain the crabmeat, reserving the liquid, and remove any
hard pieces of tendon. Set aside 2 pieces of crabmeat suitable
for decoration. Beat the eggs in a bowl, stirring in ½ teaspoon
salt, pepper to taste and the sherry. Heat 1½ tablespoons oil in
a wok or frying pan. Add the onions and mushrooms and fry
for 2 minutes, stirring all the time. Add the crabmeat and
reserved liquid and cook over a high heat for 2 to 3 minutes,
stirring continuously. Remove the pan from the heat and
allow to cool until hand-hot.

Stir the contents of the pan into the egg mixture. Heat
the remaining oil in another frying pan, pour in the mixture,
and fry over a fairly high heat until the underside begins to
turn light brown. Turn the omelet over so that the other side
sets quickly. Transfer the omelet to a hot serving dish,
sprinkle with chives or parsley, and serve garnished with the
reserved two pieces of uncooked crabmeat.

Tempura

250 g/9 oz canned bamboo
　shoots, drained
2 red peppers, seeded
2 green peppers, seeded
4 onions, sliced
400 g/14 oz frozen prawns,
　thawed
2 pieces preserved stem ginger,
　sliced

150 g/5 oz flour
50 g/2 oz rice flour
8 egg whites
300 ml/½ pint water
100 ml/4 fl oz Chinese rice wine
　or dry sherry
oil for deep frying

Cut the bamboo shoots into rounds 1 cm/½ inch thick, and cut the peppers into strips. Arrange the bamboo shoots, peppers, onions, prawns and ginger in separate small bowls. Put the flour and rice flour into a bowl. Whisk the egg whites with the water and rice wine or sherry. Stir gradually into the flour until you have a fairly liquid batter. Heat the oil in a fondue dish on the stove until it reaches a temperature of 180°C/350°F. Then put the fondue dish over its own burner.

Using a fondue fork, each guest dips his own ingredients in the batter and then deep fries them in the hot oil. Serve individual bowls of boiled rice, with a raw egg yolk broken over the top of each bowl, with this recipe. Serve soy sauce and grated white Japanese radish or horseradish in separate bowls as additional seasoning.

Sate Udang

Prawn kebabs

450 g/1 lb large frozen prawns,
　thawed
½ tablespoon soy sauce

½ teaspoon chilli sauce
1 teaspoon grated root ginger
1 teaspoon lemon juice

Cut the prawns in half lengthways. Remove the black intestinal veins if necessary and then halve them again crossways. Thoroughly mix together the remaining ingredients, add the prawns and leave to marinate for 30 minutes. Then thread the quartered prawns on to skewers and grill over a charcoal fire until cooked. Pour the liquid from the marinade over them and serve.

Curried Prawns

Ga-ti ming-hsia

150 g/5 oz canned bamboo
　shoots
10 g/⅓ oz dried Chinese
　mushrooms
225 g/8 oz frozen petits pois
450 g/1 lb frozen prawns, thawed
juice 1 lemon
1 egg white
25 g/1 oz cornflour
oil for deep frying

2 onions, chopped
ground ginger
1 green pepper, seeded and
　chopped
2 teaspoons curry powder
1 teaspoon sugar
2 tablespoons soy sauce
2 tablespoons Chinese rice wine
　or dry sherry

Drain the bamboo shoots, reserving the liquid. Cut the shoots into thin strips. Break the mushrooms into small pieces. Soak them in warm water for 15 to 30 minutes until swollen, and then drain. Meanwhile simmer the peas (still frozen) in a little water for 10 minutes, until tender. Drain and keep warm. Pat the prawns dry with absorbent paper. Trickle lemon juice over them. Beat the egg white and cornflour together, dip the prawns into this batter, and deep fry them in the oil for 2 or 3 minutes. Drain on absorbent paper and keep warm.

Heat 2 tablespoons of the frying oil in a pan. Add the onions and bamboo shoots and fry lightly. Add 150 ml/¼ pint of the reserved bamboo shoot liquid and a pinch ground ginger. Bring to the boil and simmer. Add the pepper to the pan when the onions are transparent, and stew briefly with the other vegetables. Season with the curry powder, sugar and soy sauce. Add the drained mushrooms to the pan with the prawns and peas. Warm the rice wine or sherry and pour over the dish before serving.

Curried prawns

Sambal Goreng Udang

Shrimp sambal

1 small onion, chopped
1 clove garlic, crushed
1 teaspoon ground ginger
1 teaspoon brown sugar
½ teaspoon belacan (prawn paste)
1½ teaspoons chilli sauce

2 tablespoons oil
10 peteh beans (see note below)
1 tablespoon tamarind pulp, chopped
225 g/8 oz peeled shrimps
1 bay leaf
150 ml/¼ pint coconut milk

Pound and mash together the onion, garlic, ginger, sugar, belacan (prawn paste), and chilli sauce. Heat the oil in a heavy-based pan and start to fry the mashed ingredients. Add the beans and tamarind, stir, and continue to fry for 1 minute. Stir in the shrimps and fry briefly. Add the bay leaf and coconut milk and simmer for a few minutes. Serve as a side dish.

Sambal goreng udang

Note: Peteh beans are an almond-shaped variety sold in three forms: fresh, dried, or as a kind of light pickle. The fresh beans are still in their large green pods. The dried beans have a dark brown skin that can be removed after soaking for 30 minutes in warm water. If the pickled beans are bought, their skin will generally have been removed, and the beans are a yellowish-green colour; they only need rinsing before use. As peteh beans can be difficult to obtain, they may be omitted from the recipe if unobtainable.

Chinese Shrimps

25 g/1 oz raisins
100 g/4 oz cooked ham, sliced
4 tablespoons oil
450 g/1 lb leeks, sliced
100 g/4 oz peanuts

250 ml/8 fl oz hot water
3 tablespoons soy sauce
salt, pepper
300 g/10 oz peeled shrimps

To plump up the raisins, place them in a metal sieve, pour boiling water over them and drain. Cut the ham slices into thin strips about 4 cm/1½ inches long. Heat the oil in a large pan, add the leeks and fry for 5 minutes. Then add the ham, peanuts, raisins and water and simmer for 20 minutes. Add the soy sauce. Season to taste. Finally, add the shrimps and heat through gently.

Chinese shrimps

Shrimps Chinese-style

1½ tablespoons Chinese rice wine
  or dry sherry
1½ tablespoons soy sauce
1 tablespoon cornflour
salt, ground ginger, garlic salt
300 g/10 oz canned shrimps,
  drained

20 g/¾ oz butter
450 g/1 lb frozen peas
3 tablespoons water
3 tablespoons oil
1 leek, sliced

Mix the rice wine or sherry, soy sauce, cornflour and a pinch each ground ginger and garlic salt in a cup. Place the shrimps in a dish, pour over the marinade, cover and leave to stand for 10 minutes. Meanwhile melt the butter in a pan. Add the peas (still frozen) and water, and salt lightly. Simmer, covered, for 6 minutes.

Heat the oil in a pan, add the leek and fry over high heat for 1 minute. Add the shrimps and marinade and fry for 2 minutes, stirring. Then add the peas and fry for 3 minutes longer, stirring carefully. Serve in a warmed dish.

Mow-tan-maz

Stir-fried Shrimps

1 onion, quartered
100 g/4 oz fresh bean sprouts,
  cleaned
1 large piece tender canned
  bamboo, drained
2 tablespoons oil
½ teaspoon salt
1 small piece root ginger, peeled
  and chopped

350 g/12 oz peeled shrimps
1 stick celery, chopped
2 tablespoons sake, Chinese rice
  wine or dry sherry
150 ml/¼ pint chicken stock (see
  page 6)
2 tablespoons cornflour

Cut the onion quarters lengthways into strips. Put the bean sprouts in a pan and pour on boiling water. Rinse under the cold tap until completely cooled, then drain thoroughly. Cut the bamboo lengthways into pieces 2·5 cm/1 inch thick, then cut into strips.

Heat the oil in a wok or frying pan. Add the salt and stir for 20 seconds over high heat. Add the ginger and the onion and continue stirring for 1 to 1½ minutes. Add the bamboo and bean sprouts and fry for a further 30 to 40 seconds, turning the ingredients over thoroughly in the hot oil. Add the shrimps and celery and turn a few times in the oil. Pour in the sake (or rice wine, or sherry) round the edge of the pan and stir in. Add the stock.

To thicken the sauce, mix the cornflour to a smooth paste with a little cold water in a cup. Blend a little of the hot liquid into the mixture, then return to the pan. Bring slowly to the boil and simmer gently for 2 to 3 minutes to allow the flour to cook through. Serve immediately.

Mow-tan-maz

Chinese shrimp cakes

2 small pickled cucumbers,
  drained
250 g/9 oz cornflour
2 eggs
150 ml/¼ pint water
300 ml/½ pint oil
250 g/9 oz canned chestnuts,
  drained and chopped

250 g/9 oz canned shrimps,
  drained
salt, pepper
oil for frying
sprigs parsley
juice 1 lemon

Peel the cucumbers and cut into very small dice. Mix the cornflour, eggs, water and oil to a smooth batter in a bowl. Stir in the chestnuts, shrimps and cucumber. Season to taste. Heat a little oil in a frying pan. Ladle enough batter into the pan to make a small, thin pancake 10 cm/4 inches across. Cook 3 minutes each side. Then remove from the pan, drain on absorbent paper and keep warm. Continue until all the batter is used up, adding more frying oil to the pan when necessary. Stack the pancakes on top of each other, in a warm oven, to keep warm. Serve garnished with sprigs of parsley, and with lemon juice, served separately.

POULTRY

Bebek-bumbu Bali

Balinese duck curry

2 kg/4 lb duck	2 teaspoons galingale (optional)
2 teaspoons salt	belacan (prawn paste)
2 onions, chopped	3 tablespoons oil
3 cloves garlic, crushed	3 tablespoons soy sauce
3 chilli peppers, chopped	2 pieces lemon grass (optional)
or 1½ teaspoons chilli sauce	1 bay leaf
1 teaspoon turmeric	500 ml/18 fl oz boiling water

Clean the duck and cut it into 4 pieces. Pound and mix together the salt, onions, garlic, chilli pepper or sauce, turmeric, galingale and a little belacan (prawn paste). Heat the oil in a large, heavy pan and fry the spices in it for 3 minutes. Add the duck pieces and soy sauce and continue frying until the duck pieces are brown. Add the lemon grass, bay leaf and water. Cover the pan, bring to the boil, and simmer for 40 minutes, or until the duck is tender. Stir from time to time to prevent sticking. If necessary add more hot water. When the duck is cooked, boil away as much of the liquid as possible. Transfer to a warmed dish and serve with boiled, long-grain rice.

Chinese Duck (*see pages 28–29*)

600 ml/1 pint + 5 tablespoons dry sherry	rind ½ orange
2 tablespoons honey	juice 6 oranges
2 tablespoons soy sauce	25 g/1 oz sugar
2 small pieces preserved stem ginger, chopped	1½ tablespoons cornflour
1 teaspoon mustard powder	200 g/7 oz canned mandarin oranges, drained
1 teaspoon sesame seeds	1 banana, sliced
1·5 kg/3 lb duck, ready to roast	1 orange, sliced
salt	2 cherries
40 g/1½ oz margarine	sprigs parsley

Mix the 600 ml/1 pint sherry with the honey and soy sauce. Stir in half the ginger, the mustard powder and sesame seeds. Marinate the duck in this mixture for 3 hours, covered, turning the duck from time to time. Take the duck out of the marinade, drain well and season with salt inside. Melt the margarine in a roasting pan and brown the duck on all sides. Then place the pan in the oven and roast for 1 hour 10 minutes at 200°C/400°F/gas 6, basting with the marinade every so often.

Cut the orange rind into very thin strips. Chop the remaining ginger very finely. Mix together the orange rind and juice, ginger, sugar and 2½ tablespoons sherry in a pan. Heat gently. Mix the cornflour to a smooth paste in a cup with the remaining sherry. Blend a little of the hot liquid into the mixture, then return to the pan. Bring slowly to the boil, stirring constantly. Simmer for 2 to 3 minutes to allow the flour to cook through. Then add half of the mandarin oranges and banana slices to the sauce and heat through gently.

Place the cooked duck on a warmed serving dish. Arrange the remaining mandarin oranges, and the slices of orange topped with the remaining banana slices, around the duck. Garnish with the cherries and sprigs parsley. Serve the sauce separately.

Peking Duck

1·5 kg/3 lb duck   4–5 tablespoons honey
80 ml/3 fl oz water

Peking duck is one of the most famous of all Chinese dishes; its special feature is the crisp, tasty skin which is served separately.

Ask the poulterer for a good duck, as fresh as possible. The feathers should be on, the skin as intact as possible, and the bird should still have its neck, with skin. Pluck the bird. Plunge in boiling water long enough to blanch the skin. Dry thoroughly, inside and out. Skewer or stitch up the vent firmly. Tie a piece of string under the wings and round the neck, and hang in a cool, well-ventilated place, by an open window for example, for a couple of hours until the skin is completely dry.

Bring the water to the boil and stir in the honey until fully dissolved. Leave to cool until tepid, then spread the honey mixture over the duck in several applications, pausing after each one, until the skin is impregnated with the honey. Hang the bird up again until the skin has completely dried.

Place the duck on a rack in a roasting pan. Roast until the duck is brown, 1 to 1½ hours at 190°C/375°F/gas 5. Check that the skin browns evenly; any patches that look like turning too dark should be covered with aluminium foil. The duck is then removed from the oven, and the skin is removed and carved into long, thin strips.

The correct way to eat Peking duck is with pancakes, hoisin or plum sauce and spring onion tassels (see page 77). A slice of skin and a spring onion tassel are placed on a sauce-covered pancake, which is then rolled up and eaten with the fingers.

Notes: Before being sewn up and hung to dry, the duck can be smeared inside with a paste made up of ½ teaspoon salt, ½ teaspoon hoisin, 1 teaspoon soy sauce, ½ teaspoon five-spice powder, and 1 tablespoon rice wine or sherry.

Sometimes a slit is made in the skin where the neck joins the body. A straw is inserted and air is blown under the skin so that it comes away from the flesh and balloons out. The neck is then tied with string just below the slit. This treatment makes the skin even crisper and tastier.

Traditional Peking duck is a dish which, even in China, is almost exclusively prepared by experts in restaurants where it is a speciality. Because of the specially-bred ducks, the elaborate and time-consuming preparation and special oven in which the duck should be roasted, the same sort of result should not be expected when prepared in the home.

Gano

Chicken and pork with shrimp omelet

1·5 kg/3 lb boiling chicken   4 eggs
300–400 g/10–14 oz knuckle of   1 teaspoon water
  pork   oil for frying
salt, pepper   25 g/1 oz lard
200 g/7 oz peeled shrimps   2 tablespoons soy sauce
  chopped   3 leaves white cabbage,
2 cloves garlic, crushed   shredded
2 tablespoons flour   1 celery leaf

Put the chicken and pork in a large saucepan. Season with salt and pour in enough cold water to cover. Bring to the boil, skim off the fat which rises to the surface and simmer, covered, for 2 hours, or until tender.

Pound the shrimps with half the garlic, and the salt, pepper and flour. Separately, beat the eggs with the water and season with salt. Melt a little oil in a frying pan and make 2 omelets, using half the egg mixture for each. Only allow the undersides of the omelets to set. Put half the shrimp mixture into each omelet and roll them up. Finish cooking them in a steamer, over a pan of boiling water, until set. Then leave to cool for 30 minutes and cut them across into 1 cm/½ inch slices.

Remove the chicken and pork from the stock. Strain the stock. Bone the chicken and pork and cut the meat into pieces. Melt the lard in a heavy saucepan and fry the remaining garlic. Pour in the stock and bring to the boil. Simmer for 10 minutes. Add the meat, omelet slices, soy sauce, cabbage and celery leaf, and heat through. Serve at once in warmed bowls.

Overleaf: Chinese duck

Chinese Chicken with Shrimps and Bamboo Shoots

1 kg/2 lb chicken thighs or
  breasts, boned
salt, pepper
150 g/5 oz canned bamboo
  shoots, drained
100 ml/4 fl oz oil
150 g/5 oz frozen shrimps or
  prawns, thawed
100 g/4 oz fresh mushrooms,
  sliced

900 ml/1½ pints chicken stock
  (see page 8)
1½ tablespoons cornflour
3 tablespoons soy sauce
1 teaspoon sugar
1 teaspoon sambal baatjak (see
  note below)
1 tablespoon spare rib sauce (see
  note below)
5 large prawns, peeled

Cut the chicken pieces into strips and season with salt. Cut the bamboo shoots into strips. Heat the oil in a frying pan, add the chicken and fry until golden brown (5 minutes). Add the bamboo shoots and fry for 15 minutes. Add the shrimps or prawns and mushrooms, and continue frying gently for 10 minutes, stirring from time to time.

Meanwhile make the sauce. Bring the stock to the boil in a pan. Mix the cornflour to a smooth paste with a little cold water in a cup. Blend a little of the hot stock into the mixture, then return to the pan. Bring slowly to the boil, stirring constantly. Simmer for 2 to 3 minutes to allow the flour to cook through. Season with the soy sauce, sugar, salt and pepper. Add the sauce to the chicken and shrimp mixture. Cover the pan and leave to simmer, very gently, for 5 minutes. Adjust seasoning to taste with sambal baatjak and spare rib sauce.

Serve this dish with boiled, long-grain rice. Arrange the rice in a serving dish, pour the chicken mixture into the centre and garnish with the large prawns.

Note: Sambal baatjak is an Indonesian relish and can be bought ready-prepared from oriental food shops. Spare rib sauce can also be bought ready-prepared.

Chinese chicken with shrimps and bamboo shoots

Singgang Ayam

Chicken, stewed and grilled

1 kg/2 lb chicken	½ teaspoon turmeric
1 small onion, chopped	½ teaspoon galingale (optional)
2 cloves garlic, crushed	1 teaspoon salt
½ teaspoon chilli paste	1 piece lemon grass (optional)
small slice root ginger, chopped	500 ml/18 fl oz coconut milk
½ teaspoon pepper	

The chicken for this recipe should be young, fresh and tender. Cut the chicken open down the breast. Open the two halves outwards and press flat by breaking the breast bones where they are attached to the back. Push a wooden skewer through the legs and the back so that the bird is held flat, and skewer the wings into position in the same way. Pound and mix together all the ingredients except the lemon grass and coconut milk. Rub the mixture into the chicken meat and leave for 1¼ hours to absorb the flavours.

Bring the coconut milk to the boil in a large saucepan. Add the lemon grass and chicken. Simmer over moderate heat, with the pan uncovered, until the chicken is almost done (45 minutes to 1 hour). Then remove the chicken from the pan and grill it over charcoal until golden brown. Trickle some of the cooking liquid over it from time to time. Remove the skewers and serve.

Sate Ayam

Chicken kebabs

1 kg/2 lb chicken, skinned and boned	2 cloves garlic, crushed
½ teaspoon salt	pepper
½ teaspoon belacan (prawn paste)	3 tablespoons soy sauce
	1 tablespoon lemon juice
	1 tablespoon oil

The chicken for this recipe should be young, fresh and tender. Cut the chicken meat into cubes suitable for threading on to skewers. In a basin, mash together the salt, belacan (prawn paste), garlic and a pinch pepper. Add the soy sauce and lemon juice and stir well. Add the oil and chicken pieces. Stir thoroughly and leave to marinate for 30 minutes.

Remove the chicken pieces from the marinade, drain and thread them on to small kebab skewers. Grill over a charcoal fire if possible, although an ordinary gas or electric grill will still produce good results. Baste with the marinade from time to time, and grill the kebabs until they are brown and tender. Serve immediately.

Chicken in Soy Sauce

1.5 kg/3 lb chicken, skinned and boned	1 egg white
1 tablespoon cornflour	1 leek
2 tablespoons Chinese rice wine or dry sherry	100 ml/4 fl oz oil
3 tablespoons soy sauce	500 g/18 oz canned bean sprouts, drained
	pepper, ground ginger

Cut the chicken into thin pieces about 3 cm/1¼ inches in size. Mix the cornflour in a bowl with the rice wine or sherry and 1 tablespoon soy sauce. Whisk the egg white lightly with a fork and stir into the marinade. Add the chicken pieces and allow to stand for 30 minutes.

Meanwhile cut the leek in half lengthways and then into thin strips 2 cm/¾ inch long. Heat half of the oil in a large, shallow pan. Fry the leek for 3 minutes, stirring. Add the bean sprouts and fry for another 2 minutes. Season with pepper, the remaining soy sauce and a small pinch ground ginger. Heat the remaining oil in another pan. Remove the chicken pieces from the marinade, drain and fry in the oil for 5 minutes until golden brown on all sides. Then transfer to the vegetable pan and fry for another 3 minutes, stirring all the time. Arrange on a warmed dish and serve at once.

Mo-ku-chi-pien

Stir-fried chicken with mushrooms

850 g/1¾ lb chicken thighs or
  breasts, boned
80 ml/3 fl oz Chinese rice wine or
  dry sherry
1½ tablespoons flour
salt, pepper, ground ginger
80 ml/3 fl oz oil

150 g/5 oz frozen peas, thawed
150 g/5 oz fresh button
  mushrooms
1 tablespoon soy sauce
meat extract
1 teaspoon cornflour

Cut the chicken meat into pieces and place in a bowl. Mix
together 60 ml/2 fl oz of the rice wine or sherry and the flour in
a cup. Season with salt and pepper. Pour this marinade over
the chicken pieces, cover, and leave to stand for 10 minutes.

Heat 2 tablespoons of the oil in a frying pan. Fry the peas
and mushrooms for 2 minutes, stirring. Season with salt.
Remove the vegetables from the pan and keep warm. Add the
remaining oil to the pan and heat. Stir the chicken pieces and
marinade into the pan and fry for 5 minutes, stirring all the
time. Return the vegetables to the pan and mix with the
chicken. Season to taste with salt, soy sauce, a small pinch
ground ginger and a small amount of meat extract dissolved
in a little hot water.

Mix the cornflour to a smooth paste with the remaining
rice wine or sherry and add to the pan, stirring. Let the
contents of the pan come to the boil, adjust the seasoning if
necessary, and serve.

Mo-ku-chi-pien

Chinese Fried Chicken

1 leek	ground ginger
1 kg/2 lb boiling chicken	40 g/1½ oz flour
2 tablespoons soy sauce	1 egg
2 tablespoons Chinese rice wine	oil for deep frying
or dry sherry	

Cut the leek in half lengthways and cut into thin strips. Bring a large pan of lightly salted water to the boil. Add the chicken, leek, soy sauce, 1 tablespoon rice wine or sherry and a pinch ground ginger. Simmer for 1½ hours until the chicken is tender.

Remove the chicken from the pan and drain. Reserve 4 tablespoons of the chicken stock. Remove the bones from the chicken, cut the meat into strips and allow to cool. Trickle the rest of the rice wine or sherry over the meat. While the chicken is cooling, mix the flour and egg to a smooth batter with the reserved chicken stock. Coat the chicken strips with the batter and deep fry in hot oil until golden brown. Drain on absorbent paper and serve at once.

Dembaran

Spicy chicken in coconut milk

1·5 kg/3 lb chicken	2 tablespoons tamarind pulp,
1 onion, chopped	chopped
2 cloves garlic, crushed	salt
6 almonds, chopped	3 tablespoons oil
1½ teaspoons turmeric	80 ml/3 fl oz coconut milk

Divide the chicken into 8 or 10 pieces. Pound together the onion, garlic, almonds, turmeric, tamarind and 1 teaspoon salt. Heat the oil in a flameproof casserole and fry the spices and seasonings for 3 minutes. Add the chicken pieces and brown over a moderate heat. Add the coconut milk and simmer for 45 minutes, or until the chicken is tender and the sauce has thickened. Stir from time to time to prevent sticking. Add a little extra water if necessary during cooking. Adjust seasoning and serve.

Indonesian Chicken Kebabs

4 chicken breasts (300g/10oz
  each), skinned and boned
100g/4oz chopped walnuts
300ml/½ pint lime juice or lemon
  juice
250ml/8fl oz hot chicken stock
  (see page 6)

salt, pepper
1 clove garlic
1 onion, chopped
2 tablespoons oil
150ml/¼ pint double cream
sprigs parsley

Cut the chicken into pieces suitable for threading on skewers.
Mix the walnuts, lime or lemon juice, stock, salt and pepper
in a bowl. Crush the garlic with salt and add to the marinade
with the onion. Put one third of the marinade aside and add
the chicken pieces to the remainder. Cover and allow to stand
for 3 hours.

   Drain the chicken and pat dry on absorbent paper. Thread
the chicken pieces on to skewers and brush them with the oil.

Cover the rack of the grill with aluminium foil, place the
skewers on it and grill for 20 minutes, turning once. Drain the
reserved marinade and mix with the cream to make a sauce.
Heat gently in a pan without boiling. Serve the skewers on a
warmed dish and garnish with the sprigs parsley. Serve the
sauce separately.

Right: oriental spiced chicken

Below: Indonesian chicken kebabs

Oriental Spiced Chicken

2 chickens (850g/1¾lb each)
2 teaspoons curry powder
2 teaspoons mild paprika
1 teaspoon black pepper
salt
2 tablespoons oil

4 tablespoons single cream
2 tablespoons lemon juice
1 teaspoon ground coriander
1 teaspoon ground cardamum
oil for deep frying

Cut each chicken into 4 portions. Mix together the curry powder, paprika, pepper and a pinch salt on a plate. Toss the chicken portions in this mixture and place them in a shallow dish. Stir the oil, cream and lemon juice together in a jug, and pour over the chicken pieces. Sprinkle with the coriander and cardamum. Allow to stand for 30 minutes,

turning from time to time. Remove the chicken portions from the marinade and pat dry with absorbent paper.

Heat the oil to a temperature of 180°C/350°F. Deep fry the chicken portions, in 2 batches of 4, for 15 minutes each. Keep the first batch hot while you fry the second. Arrange in a warmed dish and serve.

MEAT

Cantonese Pork

1 kg/2 lb lean pork, without skin
  or bones
1 tablespoon soy sauce
2 tablespoons chicken stock (see
  page 6)
1 tablespoon honey
1 tablespoon sugar
1 teaspoon dayong (see note
  below)
salt
2 tablespoons olive oil

Pat the pork dry with absorbent paper. Mix the soy sauce, stock, honey, sugar and dayong in a bowl. Season with salt. Spread this mixture over the pork and rub well in. Put the pork in a bowl, cover and leave to stand for 1 hour. Remove and drain, reserving the marinade. Rub the oil into the pork, put in an ovenproof dish, and paint with the reserved marinade. Cover and place on the middle shelf of the oven. Bake for 1 hour 20 minutes at 200°C/400°F/gas 6. Remove from the oven and serve in the dish with a bamboo shoot salad, boiled, long-grain rice and mushrooms.

Note: Dayong is obtainable ready-prepared from oriental food shops.

Cantonese pork

Chinese Belly of Pork

Cau Tju Juk

1 kg/2 lb lean belly of pork, with
  the rind on
garlic salt, ground star anise,
  ground ginger
1 tablespoon soy sauce
2 tablespoons groundnut oil
300 ml/½ pint hot water
1 red pepper, sliced
2 cloves star anise

SAUCE
200 g/7 oz red peppers, seeded
  and chopped
25 g/1 oz canned apricots,
  drained
1 clove garlic
salt
grated rind ½ lemon
1 tablespoon chilli sauce
2 tablespoons soy sauce

Wash and scrub the pork rind and pat dry with absorbent
paper. Make cuts across it to form a diamond pattern. Mix
together a pinch each garlic salt, ground star anise and
ground ginger in a bowl with the soy sauce and groundnut
oil. Rub this mixture well into the meat. Lay the meat on a
rack in a roasting pan, and place on the middle shelf of the
oven. Pour the water into the roasting pan and roast for 1
hour 40 minutes at 200°C/400°F/gas 6. Baste the joint from
time to time with the liquid from the pan. While the meat is
roasting, make the sauce.

  Bring a pan of lightly salted water to the boil. Add the
peppers and simmer for 20 minutes. Drain and cool slightly.
Blend the peppers with the apricots in a liquidiser, or strain
through a sieve to make a purée. Crush the garlic clove with
salt and mix into the pepper and apricot purée. Add the
lemon rind, chilli sauce and soy sauce, and mix.

  Take the meat out of the oven and arrange on a warmed
dish. Garnish with the red pepper and cloves star anise. Serve
the sauce separately with a bowl of boiled, long-grain rice.

Chinese Roast Belly of Pork

1 kg/2 lb lean belly of pork, with
  the rind on
salt
½ tablespoon brown sugar

2 tablespoons soy sauce
1 teaspoon chopped root ginger
hoisin sauce (optional)

Prick holes in the pork rind and rub well with salt. Mix
together the sugar, soy sauce, ginger and hoisin sauce if
desired. Rub this mixture into the other side of the pork.
Place the pork on a flat tray or grill pan with the rind
uppermost, and grill for 20 minutes, until the rind is crisp all
over. Transfer to the oven and roast for 1 hour at
180°C/350°F/gas 4. Remove from the oven and allow to cool
to room temperature. Cut the meat into small chunks and
serve with stir-fry Chinese cabbage (see page 75).
Watercress and spring onions are also good accompaniments
to this dish.

Below: Chinese belly of pork

Chinese roast belly of pork
with bean curd

Chinese Roast Belly of Pork with Bean Curd

½ the ingredients for Chinese
  roast belly of pork (see
  page 37)
1 cake bean curd
2–3 tablespoons soy sauce
100 ml/4 fl oz chicken stock
  (see page 6)

½ teaspoon salt
½ teaspoon sugar
1 tablespoon cornflour
2 tablespoons water
1½ tablespoons oil
sprigs parsley

Prepare and cook the roast belly of pork as described on page 37, but using half the ingredients and a shorter roasting time (about 45 minutes). Remove from the oven when cooked and allow to cool.

While the pork is cooking cut the bean curd into chunks 4 × 2 × 2 cm/1½ × ¾ × ¾ inch. When the pork has cooled cut it into similar-sized chunks. Put the soy sauce, stock, salt and sugar in a saucepan. Heat the mixture until the salt and sugar dissolve. Mix the cornflour to a smooth paste in a cup with the water.

Heat the oil in a wok or frying pan. Add the bean curd and fry, stirring, until just coloured on all sides. Pour on the soy sauce mixture and simmer over low heat for 7 minutes. Add the cornflour paste and stir, over high heat, until the sauce is thick and shiny. Add the pork to the pan and heat through. Sprinkle with parsley and serve, with boiled, long-grain rice.

Right: babi cin

Babi Cin (*see page 39*)

Spicy pork, potatoes and onions

850 g/1¾ lb fat pork	salt, pepper
2 cloves garlic, crushed	50 g/2 oz lard
small piece root ginger, chopped	250–500 ml/8–18 fl oz hot stock
or 1 teaspoon ground ginger	300 g/10 oz small potatoes
½ teaspoon ground coriander	6 baby onions, halved
1 tablespoon soy-bean paste	2 spring onions, finely chopped
2 tablespoons soy sauce	½ stick celery, finely chopped

Cut the pork (pork rashers for example) into squares. Pound and mix together the garlic, ginger, coriander and soy-bean paste. Stir in the soy sauce and season with salt and pepper. Add the meat and mix thoroughly.

Heat 25 g/1 oz lard in a saucepan, add the meat and brown on all sides. Add 250 ml/8 fl oz stock, bring to the boil, reduce the heat and simmer gently until all the fat has been drawn out.

Meanwhile heat the remaining lard in another pan. Add the potatoes and fry gently until almost done (test with a fork). Remove and keep warm. Add the baby onions to the pan in which the potatoes were cooked, and fry for a few minutes. Skim off the fat which will have risen to the top of the meat pan. Then add the potatoes and onions to the meat, pouring on more stock if necessary. Add the spring onions and celery and simmer for a further 5 minutes before serving.

Daging Masak Tomat

Meat in Tomato

450 g/1 lb pork	1 piece lemon grass (optional)
5 ripe tomatoes, skinned, seeded	½ teaspoon sugar
and chopped	1 teaspoon salt
4 red onions, chopped	300 ml/½ pint water
small piece root ginger, chopped	1 spring onion, chopped
or 2 teaspoons ground ginger	*or* 2 teaspoons chopped chives
2–3 red chilli peppers, chopped	
or 2 teaspoons chilli sauce	

Cut the pork, which should be edged with fat, into chunks. Thoroughly mix together all the remaining ingredients, except for the water and spring onion or chives. Put the mixed ingredients into a saucepan, add the water and bring to the boil. Reduce the heat and simmer gently for 45 minutes to 1 hour, until the meat is cooked and the sauce has thickened, adding a little extra water if necessary. Just before serving, stir in the spring onion or chives, allowing 1½ to 2 minutes for the spring onion to heat through, and 30 seconds for the chives. Serve immediately.

Daging masak tomat

Sweet-and-sour Pork

600 g/1¼ lb pork, cubed
oil for deep frying

MARINADE
1 egg white
40 g/1½ oz cornflour
2 tablespoons soy sauce
2 tablespoons dry sherry
salt, pepper

BATTER
1 egg
50 g/2 oz flour
150 ml/¼ pint light beer
salt

SAUCE
1 small red pepper, seeded and
  chopped
1 small green pepper, seeded and
  chopped
200 g/7 oz canned bamboo
  shoots, drained and chopped
3 canned pineapple rings,
  drained and chopped
2 tablespoons oil
600 ml/1 pint hot chicken stock
  (see page 6)
3 tablespoons soy sauce
2 tablespoons vinegar
3 tablespoons tomato ketchup
50 g/2 oz sugar
salt
20 g/¾ oz cornflour

Make the marinade first: beat the egg white in a bowl with
the cornflour. Mix in the soy sauce and sherry, and season to
taste. Put the pork cubes into the marinade and leave for 15
minutes, turning frequently.

To make the batter: whisk together the egg, flour, beer and
a pinch salt in a bowl. Remove the pork cubes from the
marinade and drain well. Dip into the batter and deep fry
them for 4 minutes, a few at a time. Remove, drain and keep
warm.

To make the sauce, heat the oil in a saucepan, and add the
peppers, bamboo shoots and pineapple. Fry, stirring, for 2
minutes. Add the stock, soy sauce, vinegar, tomato ketchup
and sugar, and stir. Season with salt and simmer for 5
minutes. Mix the cornflour to a smooth paste in a cup with a
little cold water. Blend a little of the hot liquid into the
mixture, then return to the pan. Bring slowly to the boil,
stirring constantly. Simmer for 2 to 3 minutes to allow the
flour to cook through. Arrange the pork balls on a warmed
serving dish and pour the hot sauce over.

Chinese Pork and Peas

350 g/12 oz pork fillet
100 g/4 oz frozen peas
100 ml/4 fl oz oil
150 ml/¼ pint hot stock
salt, pepper, ground ginger
sugar
1 leek
1 clove garlic, chopped
100 g/4 oz canned mushrooms,
  drained and sliced
100 g/4 oz canned bamboo
  shoots, drained and sliced
1 piece preserved stem ginger,
  sliced

1 tablespoon Chinese rice wine
  or dry sherry
1 tablespoon cornflour
2 tablespoons oyster sauce
2 teaspoons soy sauce

MARINADE
2 tablespoons soy sauce
2 teaspoons Chinese rice wine or
  dry sherry
1 egg white
1 teaspoon cornflour
salt, pepper

Slice the pork fillet thinly, cutting diagonally across the grain
of the meat. Cut the slices into strips. To make the marinade,
beat together the soy sauce, rice wine or sherry, egg white and
cornflour in a bowl. Season to taste. Put the meat into the
marinade, cover and leave to stand, preferably in the
refrigerator, for 30 minutes.

Meanwhile let the peas thaw for 5 minutes. Heat 2
tablespoons oil in a small saucepan. Add the peas and stock,
season with salt and sugar, and simmer for 5 minutes. Pour
off and reserve the stock. Keep the peas warm. Cut the leek
into strips. Heat 3 tablespoons oil in a large pan. Add the
leek, garlic, mushrooms, bamboo shoots and ginger and fry
for 5 minutes, stirring all the time. Remove from the heat and
keep warm.

Heat the remaining oil in another pan. Add the meat with
its marinade and fry for 3 minutes, stirring frequently. Add to
the vegetable pan together with the peas. Stir in the rice wine
or sherry, and the reserved stock from the peas. Mix the
cornflour to a smooth paste with the oyster sauce and soy
sauce. Stir into the pan. Bring the contents of the pan to the
boil. Season to taste with salt, pepper, ground ginger and
sugar. Serve at once.

Above: Chinese pork and peas

Babi Kecap

Pork in soy sauce

850 g/1¾ lb pork, cubed
salt, pepper
1 small onion, chopped
2 cloves garlic, crushed
small piece root ginger, chopped
1 red chilli pepper, chopped
  or ½ teaspoon chilli sauce

1 teaspoon lemon juice
2 tablespoons oil
5 tablespoons soy sauce
boiling water

Pork with some fat attached is best for this recipe. Season the
pork cubes. Mix together the onion, garlic, ginger, chilli and
lemon juice. Add the pork and leave to marinate for 10
minutes.

Heat the oil in a saucepan and lightly fry the meat and
seasonings. Add the soy sauce, stir, and pour over just enough
boiling water to cover the meat. Bring to the boil, reduce the
heat and simmer, adding more hot water if necessary, until
the meat is tender and the fat has been drawn out. The
simmering time will depend on the cut of meat. When
cooked, skim off the fat which will have risen to the surface of
the pan, adjust the seasoning and serve immediately.

Szechuan Pork

850 g/1¾ lb lean leg of pork
100 ml/4 fl oz oil
150 g/5 oz fresh mushrooms, sliced
200 g/7 oz green peppers, seeded and chopped
200 g/7 oz tomatoes, sliced

salt, ground ginger
200 g/7 oz onions, finely chopped
1 clove garlic, crushed
2 tablespoons dry sherry
300 ml/½ pint hot stock
1 tablespoon soy sauce
20 g/¾ oz cornflour

Cut the pork into thin strips 5 cm/2 inches long. Heat 4 tablespoons oil in a frying pan. Add the mushrooms, peppers and tomatoes and fry gently for 5 minutes. Remove from the pan, drain and keep warm. Heat the remaining oil in another pan. Add the meat. Sprinkle with salt and a pinch ground ginger and fry for 10 minutes, stirring. Then add the onions and garlic and fry for another 5 minutes. Pour in the sherry and heat through briefly. Then add the stock and soy sauce. Finally, add the reserved mushroom, pepper and tomato mixture. Cover the pan and stew gently over medium heat for 25 minutes.

Mix the cornflour to a smooth paste in a cup with a little cold water. Blend a little of the hot liquid into the mixture, then return to the pan. Bring slowly to the boil, stirring constantly. Simmer for 2 to 3 minutes to allow the flour to cook through. Transfer the contents of the pan to a warmed dish and serve.

Below: Szechuan pork

Chinese Liver

450g/1 lb pig's liver
flour for coating
1 red pepper, seeded
1 green pepper, seeded
200g/7oz savoy cabbage
5 tablespoons oil
salt, pepper
3 tablespoons soy sauce
2 tablespoons Chinese rice wine
  or dry sherry

200g/7oz onions, sliced
300ml/½ pint stock
150g/5oz canned bean sprouts,
  drained
  or 150g/5oz fresh bean
  sprouts, cleaned
150g/5oz canned bamboo
  shoots, drained and chopped

strips. Heat the oil in a frying pan, add the liver and brown on all sides. Remove from the pan, drain, season to taste and keep warm. Add the soy sauce and rice wine or sherry to the pan. Add the onions and simmer for 5 minutes. Add the stock, peppers and cabbage and simmer for about 10 minutes, until just tender. Return the liver to the pan. Add the bean sprouts and bamboo shoots. Reheat and serve with boiled, long-grain rice and extra soy sauce sprinkled on top if desired.

Pat the liver dry with absorbent paper and cut it into narrow strips. Toss in the flour. Cut the peppers and cabbage into

Chinese liver

Peking beef

Peking Beef

450 g/1 lb fillet of beef
5 tablespoons soy sauce
1 tablespoon Chinese rice wine
  or dry sherry
300 ml/½ pint oil
flour for coating
2 cloves garlic

salt, ground ginger, ground
  aniseed
2 leeks, finely sliced
1 tablespoon ginger syrup (from
  jar preserved stem ginger)
150 ml/¼ pint stock
1 teaspoon cornflour

Pat the meat dry with absorbent paper. Cut into very thin slices diagonally, across the grain of the meat. Mix 3 tablespoons of the soy sauce with the rice wine or sherry in a deep bowl. Add the meat, cover, and leave to marinate for 1 hour.

Heat the oil in a frying pan. Take the meat out of the marinade, drain well and dust with flour. Add to the oil and fry for 3 minutes. Remove the meat, drain and set aside. Take 4 tablespoons of the frying oil and put in another pan. Crush the garlic cloves with salt. Heat the 4 tablespoons oil, add the garlic and leeks, and fry for 5 minutes, stirring. Add the meat. Season with the ginger syrup, a pinch ground ginger, the remaining soy sauce and a small pinch ground aniseed. Pour the stock into the pan. Remove from the heat and allow to stand, covered, for 1 hour to draw out the flavours.

Return the pan to the stove and heat gently. Mix the cornflour to a smooth paste in a cup with a little cold water. Blend a little of the hot liquid into the mixture, then return to the pan. Bring slowly to the boil, stirring constantly. Simmer for 2 to 3 minutes. Adjust the seasoning, transfer to a warmed dish and serve.

Note: As an alternative to ginger syrup use honey instead, but increase the amount of ground ginger to 1 teaspoon.

Peking Breakfast

10 g/⅓ oz dried Chinese
  mushrooms
450 g/1 lb fillet of beef
1 tablespoon soy sauce
100 ml/4 fl oz water
1 teaspoon lemon juice
1 tablespoon dry sherry

4 tablespoons oil
1 leek, sliced
salt
sugar
100 g/4 oz jar mussels, drained
1 teaspoon chilli sauce

Soak the mushrooms in warm water for 15 to 30 minutes, until swollen. Meanwhile, cut the meat first into thin slices, and then into narrow strips. Mix together the soy sauce, water, lemon juice and sherry in a cup. Drain the mushrooms thoroughly.

Heat the oil in a large frying pan until it begins to smoke. Add the meat and fry, turning frequently, for 5 minutes. Add the leek and mushrooms, and continue frying, stirring all the time, for 4 minutes. Season with a pinch each salt and sugar. Add the mussels and pour the soy sauce and sherry mixture into the pan. Stir in the chilli sauce. Simmer over a very low heat for 5 minutes, then serve.

Teriyaki Steak

4 fillet steaks (200 g/7 oz each)
1 clove garlic
salt, pepper
20 g/¾ oz crystallised ginger, finely chopped
1½ tablespoons brown sugar
150 ml/¼ pint Chinese rice wine or dry sherry

100 ml/4 fl oz soy sauce
150 ml/¼ pint white wine
juice ½ lemon
4 tomatoes
50 g/2 oz canned bean sprouts, drained
1 tablespoon tomato ketchup

Teriyaki is a Japanese seasoning made on a base of soy sauce.

Pat the steaks dry with absorbent paper. Make a marinade as follows: crush the garlic with salt. Mix the garlic and ginger in a shallow bowl with the sugar, rice wine or sherry, soy sauce, white wine and lemon juice. Season with salt and pepper. Put the steaks in the marinade and turn several times. Cover and leave to stand for 12 hours. Turn from time to time during the marinating period.

Cut out any hard parts from the tomato stems. Cut a lid off the tomatoes and scoop out the seeds. Season the insides with salt and pepper. Put the bean sprouts in a pan with the tomato ketchup and heat, stirring, for 5 minutes. Stuff the tomatoes with this mixture.

Drain the steaks well. Put them on a grill rack, with the grill pan underneath, and grill 4 minutes each side. Arrange the steaks on warmed plates, garnish with the tomatoes, and serve at once with boiled, long-grain rice.

Dendeng Ragi

Stir-fried beef and coconut

450 g/1 lb lean beef
175 g/6 oz fresh coconut, grated
 or 175 g/6 oz desiccated
 coconut
1 tablespoon coriander seeds,
 crushed
1 teaspoon ground cumin
2 cloves garlic, crushed

1 small onion, chopped
salt, pepper
1 chilli pepper, chopped
 or $\frac{1}{2}$ teaspoon hot soy sauce
4 tablespoons oil
2 tablespoons hot water
2 tablespoons tamarind juice

Cut the beef across the grain into thin slices approximately
6 × 3 cm/2$\frac{1}{4}$ × 1$\frac{1}{4}$ inches. If using desiccated coconut, soak it
with 1 tablespoon water. Pound and mix together the
coriander, cumin, garlic, onion, pepper and chilli pepper or
hot soy sauce. Heat 2 tablespoons of the oil in a pan, add the
spices and fry. Add the meat slices and continue frying. Add
the coconut and hot water, and simmer over a low heat until
the moisture has been absorbed. Then add the tamarind juice
and salt, and simmer, stirring occasionally, until all the
moisture has been absorbed or evaporated, and the mixture is
as dry as possible.

   Heat the remaining oil separately. Pour this into the pan
and fry the meat and coconut over a low heat until crisp and
brown, turning from time to time to prevent the mixture
sticking. Remove the meat from the pan and drain
thoroughly on absorbent paper. Mix the fried coconut and
meat together and serve with boiled, long-grain rice.

Gadon Daging

Minced beef, steamed with spices

450 g/1 lb minced beef
2 eggs, lightly beaten
2 onions, chopped
2 cloves garlic, crushed
3 teaspoons ground coriander
$\frac{1}{2}$ teaspoon ground cumin
$\frac{1}{2}$ teaspoon ground ginger

salt, pepper
4 almonds or Brazil nuts,
 mashed
225 ml/7 fl oz coconut milk
3 pieces lemon grass (optional)
3 bay leaves

Mix together all the ingredients except the lemon grass and
bay leaves, and put in an ovenproof dish. Stick the last two
ingredients into the mixture. Place the dish in a steamer over
a pan of boiling water and steam for 30 to 40 minutes, or until
all the ingredients are cooked. Serve immediately. This recipe
can also be cooked in a bain-marie.

Dendeng ragi

Cantonese Steak

600 g/1¼ lb fillet steak, in one
  piece
3 tablespoons oil
1 piece preserved stem ginger,
  finely chopped
½ clove garlic, finely chopped
grated rind ½ orange

MARINADE
20 g/¾ oz cornflour
baking powder
1 teaspoon ginger syrup (from
  jar preserved stem ginger)
1 teaspoon fresh orange juice
1 tablespoon Chinese rice wine
  or dry sherry

1 tablespoon soy sauce
100 ml/4 fl oz water
salt
sugar
3 tablespoons groundnut or
  sesame seed oil

SAUCE
2 tablespoons tomato ketchup
1 tablespoon Chinese rice wine
  or dry sherry
2 tablespoons water
salt
sugar
Worcestershire sauce
4 drops Tabasco sauce
1 tablespoon groundnut oil

Trim off any fat or skin from the steak, pat dry with
absorbent paper and carve into 12 thin slices. Beat flat with
the ball of the hand. To make the marinade, mix the
cornflour and a small pinch baking powder in a bowl. Add
the ginger syrup, orange juice, rice wine or sherry, soy sauce
and water. Stir all together and season with salt and sugar.
Finally stir in the oil. Rub this marinade into the meat and
leave, covered, for 1 hour.

    Heat the 3 tablespoons oil in a large frying pan. Add the
ginger, garlic and orange rind to the hot oil, then add the
meat at once. Fry on each side for 2 minutes. Remove from
the pan and keep hot on a warmed dish.

    To make the sauce: add the tomato ketchup, rice wine or
sherry, and water to the hot oil in the pan and mix. Season to
taste with salt, sugar, Worcestershire sauce and the Tabasco
sauce. Put the steaks back in the sauce, stir in the last
tablespoon of oil, and heat through. Serve immediately in a
warmed dish.

Chinese Steak with Green Peppers

450 g/1 lb rump steak
1½ tablespoons cornflour
2 tablespoons dry sherry
3 tablespoons soy sauce
1 tablespoon sugar
salt, ground ginger

salt, ground ginger
oil for frying
2 green peppers, seeded and
  chopped

Cut the steak into thin slices. Trim off any fat and cut each
slice into four. Mix the cornflour, sherry, soy sauce, sugar
and a pinch ground ginger in a bowl. Turn the pieces of meat
in this marinade, cover, and leave to stand, preferably in the
refrigerator, for 3 hours to absorb the flavours, turning from
time to time.

    Heat the oil to a very high temperature in a large frying
pan. Remove the meat from the marinade, pat it dry with
absorbent paper, and fry for 5 minutes, shaking the pan to
prevent the meat sticking. Remove from the pan, drain and
transfer to a warmed serving dish. Keep warm. Add the
peppers to the pan and fry for 5 minutes. Season with salt.
Remove from the pan, drain and use to garnish the meat.
Serve at once.

Tokyo Steak

4 fillet steaks (150 g/5 oz each)
1 tablespoon green peppercorns
2 tablespoons Chinese rice wine
  or dry sherry
salt, ground ginger

butter for frying
325 g/11 oz canned mandarin
  oranges, drained
20 g/¾ oz butter, cut into flakes

Pat the steaks dry with absorbent paper. Mix the peppercorns
and rice wine or sherry in a bowl. Season with salt and
ground ginger. Rub this mixture well into the steaks. Heat
the butter in a frying pan. Add the steaks and fry for 2
minutes each side. Remove the steaks from the pan and
arrange them on a grill rack, with the grill pan underneath to
catch the drips. Place the mandarin oranges on top of the
steaks and scatter on the flakes of butter. Grill for 3 minutes.
Arrange the steaks on a warmed serving plate and serve with
fried bean sprouts, boiled, long-grain rice and sake.

Tokyo steak

Sate Padang

Padang-kebabs

1 teaspoon salt
450 g/1 lb beef, cubed
1 onion, chopped
2 cloves garlic, crushed
1 teaspoon chilli sauce
small piece root ginger,
  chopped
½ teaspoon galingale (optional)

½ teaspoon pepper
1 teaspoon turmeric
½ teaspoon ground coriander
1 teaspoon ground cumin
2 pieces lemon grass (optional)
2 tablespoons rice flour
  or 2 tablespoons cornflour

Rub the salt into the meat cubes. Pound and mix together the onion, garlic, chilli sauce, ginger, galingale, pepper, turmeric, coriander and cumin. Put three quarters of this spicy marinade into a saucepan. Add the meat and stir. Allow to stand for 15 minutes so that the meat absorbs all the flavours. Then add just enough water to cover the meat. Bring to the boil, reduce the heat, add the lemon grass and simmer, with the pan partly covered, until the meat is nearly cooked but still firm.

Remove the meat from the pan and allow to drain. Add the remaining marinade to the pan and continue to simmer. Carefully thread the pieces of meat on to small kebab skewers and finish cooking by grilling, preferably over charcoal, until well browned. Baste occasionally with the marinade sauce during the cooking.

Mix the rice flour or cornflour to a smooth paste in a cup with a little cold water. Blend a little of the hot marinade into the mixture, then return to the pan. Bring slowly to the boil, stirring constantly. Simmer for 2 to 3 minutes to allow the flour to cook through. Arrange the meat on warmed plates, pour the sauce over and serve as part of a Malaysian or Indonesian-style dinner.

Note: Great care should be taken not to let the meat get too tender at the braising stage, as it still has to be grilled.

Mongolian Fondue

850g/1¾lb tender beef

CHICKEN BROTH

1·5 litres/2½ pints chicken stock (see page 6)
2 carrots, sliced
1 leek, sliced
¼ celeriac root, chopped
1 tablespoon chopped parsley

TARTARE SAUCE

100g/4oz mayonnaise
2 tablespoons small capers
2 tablespoons chopped chives
2 pickled gherkins, finely chopped
2 teaspoons lemon juice

2 tablespoons canned evaporated milk
salt, pepper
sugar

KETCHUP SAUCE

100g/4oz mayonnaise
2 tablespoons tomato ketchup
1 teaspoon Worcestershire sauce
sambal (see note below)
curry sauce
sugar
salt

Pat the meat dry with absorbent paper. Cut into thin slices, about the thickness of sliced salami. Bring the chicken stock to the boil on the stove, in the fondue dish. Add the carrots, leek, celeriac and parsley, and simmer for 20 minutes.

To make the tartare sauce, mix the mayonnaise with the capers, chives, gherkins and lemon juice. Stir in the evaporated milk until the sauce is creamy. Season to taste with salt, pepper and a pinch sugar.

To make the ketchup sauce, mix together the mayonnaise, tomato ketchup and Worcestershire sauce. Stir in a small amount of sambal and a dash of curry sauce. Season to taste with a pinch each sugar and salt.

Arrange the meat, tartare sauce and ketchup sauce in separate bowls on the table. Place the chicken broth, simmering gently in the fondue dish, over its flame on the table. As it evaporates, top it up with boiling water. Each guest wraps a slice of meat round his fondue fork, dips it into the simmering broth, and leaves it there for at least 1 minute to cook the beef through. The meat is then dipped into the sauces and eaten. Serve with boiled, long-grain rice.

Note: Sambal is an Indonesian relish, available ready-prepared, in several different varieties, from oriental food shops.

Chinese Fondue

850g/1¾lb fillet steak (or use half each pork and veal fillet)
1 litre/1¾ pints good beef stock

2 tablespoons white wine or whisky
3 teaspoons soy sauce

Remove all fat and white skin from the meat. Cut into thin slices, about the thickness of sliced salami, and arrange on plates in individual portions. Heat the stock on the stove in the fondue dish. Flavour it with the white wine or whisky, and soy sauce. Put the fondue dish over its flame in the centre of the table. Every guest spears a slice of meat on his fondue fork, dips it into the boiling stock and lets it cook for 1 minute. The meat is then dipped into various spicy accompaniments and sauces (see below) before being eaten. When all the meat has been eaten, the stock in which it was cooked is poured into small cups and drunk as a soup.

Good accompaniments to a Chinese fondue are well-flavoured sauces such as curry-flavoured mayonnaise, rémoulade sauce, apple and horseradish cream, fruits in mustard pickle, small pickled onions and sweet-and-sour gherkins. They can be bought ready-prepared or made at home.

Mongolian fondue

Sate Bali

Balinese kebabs

4 shallots, chopped
  or 4 baby onions, chopped
3 cloves garlic, crushed
1 piece lemon grass (optional)
small piece root ginger, chopped
  or ½ teaspoon ground ginger
1 teaspoon ground coriander
1 teaspoon belacan (prawn
  paste)
  or 1 tablespoon shrimps
1 teaspoon tamarind pulp
  or 1 date, finely chopped
½ chilli pepper, finely chopped
  or ½ teaspoon chilli sauce

½ teaspoon turmeric or ½
  teaspoon curry powder
2 teaspoons salt
juice ½ lemon
250 g/9 oz pork fillet, cubed
250 g/9 oz lamb from leg or
  shoulder, cubed
2 tablespoons oil
2 tablespoons coconut milk
butter
1 tablespoon soy sauce

Pound and mix together the shallots, garlic, lemon grass, ginger, coriander, belacan, tamarind, chilli, turmeric and salt. Stir in the lemon juice. Add the meat, stir well, and leave to marinate for at least 1 hour. Remove the meat from the marinade and drain, reserving the marinade. Thread the meat on to small skewers (about 5 pieces to a skewer) and brush with oil. Barbecue over a charcoal fire, or grill on a rack under the grill, with the grill pan underneath to catch the drips, turning from time to time. Baste with the oil during cooking.

The left-over marinade can be used for an accompanying sauce, thinned with the coconut milk and, if necessary, a knob of butter and the soy sauce. This mixture is heated up and served separately in a small bowl.

Oriental Fondue

Chu-bua-buo

SERVES 6

225 g/8 oz pork fillet
225 g/8 oz fillet of beef
225 g/8 oz calves' liver
225 g/8 oz fillets of sole
175 g/6 oz chicken breast,
  skinned and boned
450 g/1 lb celery
100 g/4 oz transparent noodles
2 tablespoons soy sauce

2 tablespoons oil
2 tablespoons Chinese rice wine
  or dry sherry
3 eggs
225 g/8 oz spinach, washed and
  picked over
2 litres/3½ pints chicken stock
  (see page 6)

Pat the pork, beef, liver, fish and chicken dry with absorbent paper. Place in the freezing compartment of the refrigerator for 30 minutes; this will enable you to cut them very thin with a sharp knife. Cut them into strips 8 cm/3¼ inches long and 2 cm/¾ inch wide. Cut the celery into similar-sized strips,

blanch in boiling water for 4 minutes, drain and pat dry. Soak the noodles for 30 minutes in warm water. Drain and cut into pieces 10 cm/4 inches long.

Make a sauce as follows: beat together the soy sauce, oil, rice wine or sherry and eggs. Put 1 tablespoon into a small bowl for each person. Arrange the meat, fish, prawns, noodles, celery and spinach in small bowls and place on the table. Heat the chicken stock to boiling point, pour into a fondue dish or other flameproof container, and stand over a burner in the centre of the table.

Lay the table with a fondue fork and an empty bowl for each person. Each guest puts some meat in his bowl, spikes it on his fork and cooks it for 1 minute in the chicken stock. When it is done he dips it into his sauce and eats it. The meat and fish are eaten first, which gives the chicken stock added flavour. Then the noodles and vegetables are boiled for 1 minute in the remaining stock. Each guest has a portion, and can dip his noodles and vegetables in any sauce he has left.

Chinese Hotpot

Ho Go

SERVES 6

6 eggs
80 ml/3 fl oz soy sauce
4 chicken breasts, skinned
  and boned
4 chicken livers
225 g/8 oz fillet steak
225 g/8 oz pork fillet
300 g/10 oz canned bamboo
  shoots, drained

2 leeks, sliced
225 g/8 oz frozen prawns,
  thawed
225 g/8 oz fresh mushrooms,
  sliced
225 g/8 oz fresh bean sprouts,
  cleaned
1·5 litres/2½ pints chicken stock
  (see page 6)

Whisk together the eggs and soy sauce; divide this mixture between six bowls, placing one at each place setting. Cut the chicken breasts and livers into thin strips. Cut the fillet steak and pork fillet into thin slices the thickness of sliced salami. Cut the bamboo shoots into thin strips. Blanch the leeks in hot water and drain. Put these ingredients, and the prawns, mushrooms and bean sprouts, into bowls and arrange on the table. Heat the chicken stock on the stove in a fondue dish. When it has come to the boil place the dish over its burner in the centre of the table.

Each guest helps himself to a selection of raw ingredients from the bowls on the table. Using a fondue fork, he then spikes one or more items, dips it into the boiling stock and leaves it there until cooked. He then dips it into his bowl of egg and soy sauce before eating it. When all the raw ingredients have been eaten, the stock is poured into the bowls containing the remains of the egg and soy sauce, stirred around and drunk as soup.

RICE, NOODLES AND DUMPLINGS

The cookery of North China is famous for noodle dishes. Noodles are considered a symbol of longevity in China – hence why they are nearly all very long. The types usually found in oriental supermarkets in Europe are transparent noodles, made of pea-starch or rice flour, and Chinese noodles made of wheat flour. Rice dishes are more common in South China. Long-grain rice is most often used.

Special Fried Rice

200 g/7 oz long-grain rice
200 g/7 oz cooked ham
3 tablespoons oil
150 g/5 oz canned prawns or shrimps, drained
2 tablespoons soy sauce
1 leek, sliced
4 eggs, beaten
salt, pepper

Bring a pan of salted water to the boil. Add the rice and cook at a fast boil for 10 minutes. Drain in a sieve, rinse under the cold tap and drain again. Cut the ham into strips. Heat the oil in a pan. Fry the ham and prawns or shrimps for 5 minutes, stirring all the time. Add the rice and soy sauce and fry for another 5 minutes. Add the leek and fry for a further 5 minutes. Season the beaten eggs and stir into the pan until they scramble. Arrange on a warmed dish and serve.

Special fried rice

Special Egg Fried Rice

40 g/1½ oz dried Chinese black
  fungus
150 g/5 oz long-grain rice
100 g/4 oz frozen peas, thawed
  and drained
75 g/3 oz canned bamboo
  shoots, drained and cut into
  strips
250 g/9 oz cold roast chicken, cut
  into strips

60 g/2½ oz peeled prawns
4 tablespoons oil
75 g/3 oz canned bean sprouts,
  drained
3 eggs
4 tablespoons soy sauce
1 tablespoon Chinese rice wine
  or dry sherry
cayenne
sugar

Soak the fungus in warm water for 15 to 30 minutes, until
swollen. Drain thoroughly. Meanwhile, bring a pan of
salted water to the boil, add the rice and simmer for 10
minutes. Drain the rice, rinse under the cold tap, and drain
again thoroughly. Drain the fungus. Place the rice in a large
bowl and carefully mix in the fungus, peas, bamboo shoots,
chicken and prawns.

Heat the oil in a large frying pan until very hot. Add the
rice mixture and fry, stirring, for 10 minutes. Then add the
bean sprouts. Beat the eggs with the soy sauce, and rice wine
or sherry. Season with a pinch each cayenne and sugar. Pour
this mixture over the rice. Allow the eggs to thicken slightly,
stirring with a spatula from time to time. Serve immediately.

Special egg fried rice

Indonesian Rijstaffel *(see pages 56–57)*

SERVES 10

This is the famous national dish of Indonesia, served in top-
class restaurants all over the world, and highly praised by
gourmets. It comes originally from Java. Rijstaffel is a Dutch
word meaning, literally, 'rice table'. Because of the number of
different dishes involved, it takes quite some time to prepare.
For a special meal you should aim for a mixture of 9 or 10
dishes, some hot and some cold. For an ordinary family meal
you can serve fewer dishes. All the different dishes are
arranged on the table and each guest helps himself to
whatever he fancies.

To be served cold:

ROASTED COCONUT

100 g/4oz coconut, coarsely
  grated
50 g/2oz peanuts

1 teaspoon sugar
salt

Mix together in a bowl the coconut, peanuts and sugar.
Season to taste with salt. Brown in a hot frying pan for 5
minutes, stirring all the time. Put into a small bowl for serving.

ROASTED PEANUTS

225 g/8oz peanuts
salt

1 tablespoon coconut oil

Sprinkle the peanuts with salt. Heat the oil in a frying pan,
add the peanuts and fry over a moderate heat for 10 minutes,
until golden brown. Put into a small bowl for serving.

KROEPOEK

oil for deep frying
1 packet kroepoek

Kroepoek is pounded dried shrimp mixed with tapioca flour,
and pressed into dry slices. It can be bought in oriental food
shops. The slices are about 4cm/1½ inches in size, and swell up
to twice that size in the hot fat. Fry only 2 or 3 pieces at a
time.

Heat the oil in a large pan. Deep fry the pieces of kroepoek,
2 or 3 at a time, but do not let them brown or they will lose
their flavour. Arrange on a dish for serving.

Note: The following should also be served cold. You will
need 2 or 3 kinds of sambal (Indonesian relishes made of
pounded or crushed ingredients). For instance, sambal oelek
(very hot), sambal badjak and sambal goreng. Other suitable
accompaniments are small pickled gherkins, sliced cooked
beetroot, small pickled onions, and canned sweet-and-sour
ginger. There should also be 1 hard-boiled egg per person,
cut into slices, and slices of cold roast chicken. The eggs and
chicken slices are covered with a sambal sauce (see recipe
on page 55).

½ clove garlic
salt
3 tablespoons coconut oil
1 shallot, chopped
2 almonds, chopped
2 small red peppers, seeded and chopped

¼ bay leaf
150 ml/¼ pint tamarind liquid *or* 150 ml/¼ pint strong chicken stock
150 ml/¼ pint fresh coconut milk
sugar

Crush the garlic with salt. Heat the oil in a pan, add the shallot, garlic, almonds and peppers, and fry for 5 minutes, until brown. Add the bay leaf, tamarind liquid or chicken stock, and coconut milk. Bring to the boil, stirring, and continue to boil for 1 minute. Season to taste with salt and sugar. Allow to cool. Arrange the hard-boiled egg and chicken slices (see note on page 54) on a plate; pour the sauce over before serving.

To be served hot:

CURRY SOUP

1 clove garlic
salt, ground coriander
3 tablespoons oil
3 small red peppers, seeded and chopped
3 small green peppers, seeded and chopped
5 shallots, chopped
1 teaspoon ground cumin

1 teaspoon ground ginger
1 kg/2 lb chicken, skinned and boned
40 g/1½ oz butter
450 g/1 lb canned celery, drained and chopped
1 bay leaf
1·5 litres/2½ pints hot water
juice 1 lemon

The original version of this recipe uses an Indian vegetable called seré instead of the celery; you may be able to find it canned in shops specialising in exotic foods.

Crush the garlic with salt. Heat the oil in a pan. Add the peppers, shallots, garlic, cumin and a pinch coriander, and fry gently for a few minutes, stirring. Add the ginger. Fry for 15 minutes, until brown. Put the mixture through a sieve or liquidise it, and put aside. Cut the chicken into pieces about 4 cm/1½ inches in size. Heat the butter in a large pan, add the chicken and fry gently on all sides for 15 minutes, until browned. Add the celery, bay leaf, reserved purée and water, and simmer for 30 minutes, until the chicken is tender. Season to taste with the lemon juice and salt, remove the bay leaf, and keep warm until needed.

INDIAN CHICKEN CURRY

1·5 kg/3 lb chicken
50 g/2 oz butter
1 onion, chopped
2 teaspoons flour
1 tablespoon curry powder
2 teaspoons curry paste
400 ml/¾ pint white stock
1 apple, peeled and chopped

2 teaspoons mango chutney
1 tablespoon lemon juice
salt, pepper
25 g/1 oz sultanas
25 g/1 oz blanched almonds
2 teaspoons desiccated coconut
2 tablespoons cream
1 banana, sliced

Divide the chicken into neat joints. Melt the butter in a large pan, add the chicken and fry until lightly browned. Remove from the pan, drain and keep warm. Add the onion and fry until golden. Add the flour, curry powder and curry paste and fry well, stirring occasionally. Stir in the stock and bring to the boil. Return the chicken joints to the pan and add all the remaining ingredients except the cream and banana. (The coconut should be tied in muslin and removed after 15 minutes.) Simmer gently for 1¼ hours, adding a little more stock if necessary.

Remove the chicken pieces from the pan, drain and keep warm. Stir the cream into the sauce and put aside. Before serving reheat the sauce and pour over the chicken pieces. Garnish with banana slices.

SATCH

Small meat kebabs, prepared according to the recipe for Sate Bali (see page 52). Keep warm until needed.

MEAT DUMPLINGS

1 clove garlic
salt
450 g/1 lb minced beef
5 tablespoons cold water
1 teaspoon ground coriander
1 teaspoon ground cumin

1 onion, chopped
dried mint
50 g/2 oz coconut fat
300 ml/½ pint hot stock
1 teaspoon curry powder
1 tablespoon cornflour

Crush the garlic with salt. Mix the beef and water together in a pan until you have a thick mass. Heat gently for 5 minutes, stirring. Remove from the heat, add the coriander, cumin, onion, garlic and a pinch dried mint, and mix well. Knead into a doughy consistency. Season with salt if desired. Wet the hands and form the mixture into small dumplings 2 cm/¾ inch across. Heat the coconut fat in a pan, add the dumplings and fry for 10 minutes, until browned. Transfer to a dish and keep warm.

To make the sauce, add the stock to the remaining fat and meat juices in the pan. Stir in the curry powder. Mix the cornflour to a smooth paste in a cup with a little cold water. Blend a little of the hot liquid into the mixture, then return to the pan. Bring slowly to the boil, stirring constantly. Simmer for 2 to 3 minutes to allow the flour to cook through. Adjust the seasoning and put aside. Just before serving reheat the sauce and pour over the dumplings.

FRIED SHRIMPS

450 g/1 lb frozen shrimps or prawns, thawed
2 egg yolks

40 g/1½ oz breadcrumbs
5 tablespoons coconut oil

Press the shrimps or prawns flat, coat with egg yolk and then with breadcrumbs. Heat the oil in a pan and fry the shrimps or prawns for 10 minutes, until brown. Keep warm until needed.

Note: You should also serve hot a large bowl of boiled, long-grain rice (450 g/1 lb) and a bowl of banana slices fried in butter (use 6 bananas).

Overleaf: Indonesian rijstaafel

Right: Javanese rice

Left: Indonesian rice salad

Indonesian Rice Salad

100 g/4 oz long-grain rice
2 tablespoons oil
1 onion, finely chopped
1 tablespoon curry powder
250 g/9 oz cold roast chicken,
  cut into strips
1 apple, peeled, cored and
  chopped
1 orange, divided into segments,
  pith and skin removed, and
  chopped
1 banana, peeled and chopped
½ fennel bulb, trimmed and
  chopped
1 red pepper, seeded and
  chopped

1 chilli pepper, seeded and
  chopped
1 piece preserved stem ginger,
  chopped

DRESSING
juice 1 lemon
4 tablespoons tomato ketchup
1–2 teaspoons Pernod
4 tablespoons mayonnaise
2 tablespoons soured cream

GARNISH
50 g/2 oz flaked almonds,
  toasted
1 orange, sliced
8 maraschino cherries

Bring a pan of salted water to the boil. Add the rice, reduce the heat and simmer for 15 minutes, until tender. Drain the rice, rinse under the cold tap, and drain again thoroughly.

Heat the oil in a pan and fry the onion gently for 5 minutes, until soft. Remove the pan from the heat and stir in the curry powder and rice. Turn the contents of the pan into a bowl, and mix in the chicken, fruit, vegetables and ginger.

To make the dressing, mix the lemon juice, tomato ketchup, Pernod, mayonnaise and cream in a bowl. Pour three quarters of the dressing on to the rice mixture and mix in thoroughly. Allow to stand for 1 hour.

To serve, arrange the rice salad in 4 separate bowls. Pour the remaining dressing over the 4 salads, and garnish with the nuts, orange slices and cherries.

Javanese Rice

225 g/8 oz long-grain rice
50 g/2 oz butter or margarine
4 chicken legs weighing
  850 g/1¾ lb altogether, skinned,
  boned and sliced
200 g/7 oz peeled shrimps
2 red peppers, seeded and
  chopped

1 piece preserved stem ginger
50 g/2 oz flaked almonds
1 teaspoon curry powder
ground ginger
1 small jar (220 g/7¾ oz) Chinese
  or Italian fruits pickled with
  mustard, drained

Wash the rice thoroughly under the cold tap and drain. Bring a pan of salted water to the boil, add the rice and simmer gently for 15 minutes.

Meanwhile melt the butter or margarine in a large pan. Fry the chicken slices on all sides for 5 minutes, until lightly browned. Add the shrimps and peppers and continue frying for another 5 minutes, stirring all the time. Cut the piece of ginger into quarters and then into very thin slices. Add to the pan with the almonds and continue frying for a further 3 minutes. Drain the rice in a sieve, rinse with warm water and drain again. Add the rice to the pan and heat through, stirring. Season with the curry powder and a small pinch ground ginger. Stir in the fruits and serve.

Nasi Goreng

Indonesian fried rice

SERVES 8

600 g/1¼ lb boiling chicken, quartered
1 litre/1¾ pints water
salt, pepper
400 g/14 oz long-grain rice
1 red pepper, seeded
100 ml/4 fl oz oil
4 onions, chopped
3 cloves garlic, chopped
300 g/10 oz canned crabmeat, drained

250 g/9 oz cooked ham
600 g/1¼ lb canned prawns or large shrimps, drained
3 eggs, beaten
1 teaspoon sambal oelek (an Indonesian relish)
curry powder, ground ginger, ground cumin, ground coriander, ground nutmeg, powdered saffron (or turmeric)

Place the chicken pieces in a large, heavy saucepan. Cover generously with water and bring to the boil. Skim off any froth or bits which rise to the surface. Reduce the heat and simmer, covered, for 1 hour or until tender.

Remove the chicken pieces from the stock and allow to cool. Then remove the skin and bones from the chicken, cut the flesh into small pieces and set aside. Put the chicken stock in a pan, add the 1 litre/1¾ pints water and a pinch salt, and bring to the boil. Meanwhile wash the rice until the water runs clear. Add the rice to the boiling liquid and simmer for 12 minutes over low heat, until the rice grains have swelled but are not completely cooked. Drain in a sieve, pour warm water over the rice to rinse it, and drain again. Cut the pepper into narrow strips.

Heat 80 ml/3 fl oz of the oil in a large pan. Add the onions, garlic and pepper and stew gently for 5 minutes. Add the rice. Continue cooking very gently for 10 minutes, stirring frequently. Remove any horny strips from the crabmeat. Cut the ham into strips. Add the crabmeat, ham, prawns or shrimps and chicken to the pan and mix. Heat the remaining oil in another pan. Add the eggs and scramble, stirring. Mix the sambal oelek and spices to taste in a cup with a little water. Add to the rice mixture with the scrambled egg and stir. Leave over a very low heat for 10 minutes, stirring occasionally. Transfer the mixture to a warmed dish and serve.

Note: Nasi goreng should be served with a selection of spicy sauces and side dishes. These can be prepared beforehand or bought ready-made. Suitable accompaniments would be: sweet peppers in an oil and vinegar dressing; pineapple chunks; pickled cucumber; chilli sauce; mixed pickles; mustard pickles; mango chutney; tomato ketchup; soy sauce; fried sliced banana; crystallised ginger; roasted peanuts or cashew nuts and any Indonesian relish available.

Nasi goreng

Congee

Chinese rice porridge

100 g/4 oz long-grain rice
1 litre/1¾ pints water
1 tablespoon dried shrimps,
  washed
small piece orange rind

small piece leftover roast pork
  or duck, finely chopped
½ tablespoon dry sherry
2 tablespoons finely chopped
  spring onion or chives

Put the rice and water in a saucepan. Add the shrimps and orange rind and bring quickly to the boil. Reduce the heat, cover the pan and simmer for 45 minutes. Add the pork or duck and sherry, and simmer gently for another hour. Stir from time to time and add more water if necessary; the rice porridge should not become too thick. Serve in individual bowls, sprinkled with the spring onion or chives, as a lunchtime snack.

Bami Kuah

Fried noodles with chicken and pork

225 g/8 oz Chinese egg noodles
$3\frac{1}{2}$ tablespoons oil
$\frac{1}{2}$ chicken (750 g/$1\frac{1}{2}$ lb)
250 g/9 oz pork
salt, pepper
1 litre/$1\frac{3}{4}$ pints water
50 g/2 oz fresh button
  mushrooms
1 clove garlic, crushed
1 teaspoon finely chopped
  root ginger
  or $\frac{1}{2}$ teaspoon ground ginger

1 small leek, sliced
1 tablespoon finely chopped
  celery
1 tablespoon soy sauce
3 tablespoons crisply fried
  onions
3 tablespoons chopped
  chives

Cook the noodles until tender as indicated on the packet. Drain in a sieve, rinse under the cold tap and drain again thoroughly. Then turn them in $\frac{1}{2}$ tablespoon of the oil. Put the chicken and pork in a saucepan and season. Add the water and bring to the boil. Skim the liquid, reduce the heat, cover the pan and leave to simmer for 15 to 20 minutes. Remove the chicken and pork from the saucepan, skin and bone the chicken, then slice both the chicken and pork thinly. Strain the stock and keep hot.

Heat 2 tablespoons of the oil in a pan and fry the mushrooms for 1 minute. Add the chicken and pork and turn in the hot fat for a further minute. Remove everything from the pan and keep hot. Heat the remaining oil in the pan and fry the garlic and ginger for 1 minute. Remove and add to the other ingredients being kept hot. Then fry the leek and celery in the fat for 2 to 3 minutes. Return the chicken, pork, mushrooms, garlic and ginger to the pan, pour over the hot stock and soy sauce. Add a little more salt to taste. Stir in the noodles and heat through. Serve in large bowls garnished with the onions and chives.

Bami Goreng

Fried Noodles

450 g/1 lb Chinese noodles
3–4 tablespoons oil
2 red onions, finely chopped
1 small leek, sliced
1 clove garlic, crushed
350 g/12 oz roast pork, chopped
1 teaspoon finely chopped
  root ginger
  or $\frac{1}{2}$ teaspoon ground ginger
salt, pepper
4 spring onions, chopped

1 tablespoon finely chopped
  celery
225 g/8 oz peeled shrimps
1 tablespoon soy sauce
2 tablespoons chicken or other
  stock
1 tablespoon crisply fried onions
$\frac{1}{2}$ tablespoon finely chopped
  parsley
2 eggs, beaten

Cook the noodles as indicated on the packet. Drain in a sieve, rinse under the cold tap and drain again thoroughly. Then turn in $\frac{1}{2}$ tablespoon of the oil.

Heat 2 to 3 tablespoons of the remaining oil in a large frying pan. Add the red onions, leek and garlic, and fry until golden brown. Add the meat and ginger, season, and fry together, stirring, for a few minutes. Add the spring onions, celery and shrimps, and fry for a further 1 to $1\frac{1}{2}$ minutes over medium heat. After adding a little more oil if necessary, put the noodles in the pan. Fry over high heat, stirring constantly, for 2 minutes, or until they are fully heated through and lightly fried. Stir in the soy sauce and stock. Transfer to a warmed dish, garnish with the onions and parsley, and keep hot.

Quickly cook a thin omelet with the eggs. Cut the omelet into 1 cm/$\frac{1}{2}$ inch strips, make a lattice pattern over the noodles and serve

Chop Suey

450 g/1 lb lean pork
2 tablespoons Chinese rice wine
  or dry sherry
4 tablespoons soy sauce
salt, pepper, ground ginger
50 g/2 oz transparent noodles
50 g/2 oz celery
1 tablespoon dried Chinese
  black fungus
75 g/3 oz canned bamboo shoots,
  drained

100 ml/4 fl oz groundnut oil
2 onions, chopped
150 g/5 oz canned bean sprouts,
  drained
100 g/4 oz fresh mushrooms,
  sliced
1 teaspoon sugar
1½ tablespoons cornflour
60 ml/2 fl oz dry sherry

Cut the pork into thin strips. Mix the rice wine or sherry and 2 tablespoons soy sauce in a bowl. Season with salt, pepper and a pinch ground ginger. Add the pork strips to the marinade, cover and allow to stand for 1 hour. Meanwhile break up the noodles into small pieces. Bring a pan of lightly salted water to the boil, add the noodles and simmer for 5 minutes. Rinse under the cold tap, drain and put aside. Cut the celery into short strips and blanch for 5 minutes in boiling, lightly salted water. Remove and drain. Soak the dried black fungus in warm water for 30 minutes, drain and cut into fairly large pieces. Cut the bamboo shoots into strips.
Put the oil in a large frying pan and heat it until very hot.

Remove the pork from the marinade, drain well and fry in the oil for 2 minutes. Remove and keep warm. Add the onions, bamboo shoots, bean sprouts, fungus and fresh mushrooms. Fry for 3 minutes. Mix in the pork, celery and noodles. Season with the remaining soy sauce and the sugar. Simmer for another 3 minutes, stirring gently.

Mix the cornflour to a smooth paste in a cup with the sherry. Add to the pan and bring slowly to the boil, stirring constantly. Simmer for 2 to 3 minutes to allow the flour to cook through. Adjust the seasoning and serve at once with boiled, long-grain rice.

Fried Noodles with Pork

225 g/8 oz pork fillet
100 ml/4 fl oz soy sauce
4 tablespoons Chinese rice wine or dry sherry
225 g/8 oz Chinese noodles
100 ml/4 fl oz groundnut oil
10 g/⅓ oz dried Chinese mushrooms
150 g/5 oz leek
225 g/8 oz canned bamboo shoots, drained
150 g/5 oz cooked ham
salt
1 teaspoon mild paprika
ground ginger

Slice the pork thinly against the grain of the meat. Cut the slices into strips and place in a bowl. Mix together 2 tablespoons each of the soy sauce and rice wine or sherry. Pour over the meat and leave to marinate for 30 minutes, turning from time to time.

Meanwhile, bring a pan of salted water to the boil, add the noodles and cook at a fast boil for 3 to 4 minutes. They should be tender but not quite cooked. Rinse in a sieve under the cold tap and drain. Place in a warmed dish with 1 tablespoon of the oil. Keep warm. Break up the mushrooms slightly, pour boiling water over them and leave to soak for 10 minutes. Meanwhile cut the leek into halves or quarters, according to its thickness, then cut into strips 3 cm/1¼ inches long. Cut the bamboo shoots and ham into similar-sized strips. Remove the mushrooms from the water and drain.

Heat 3 tablespoons of the oil in a large pan. Remove the pork strips from the marinade, reserving the marinade. Drain the pork and add to the hot oil. Fry briefly, stirring so that the meat does not stick. Add the leek, bamboo shoots, ham and mushrooms. Fry for 4 minutes, stirring. Pour in the reserved marinade and bring to the boil. Remove from the heat immediately, transfer to a warmed dish and keep warm.

Clean out the frying pan. Heat the remaining oil, add the noodles and fry for 10 minutes. Season lightly with salt. Mix together the paprika, a pinch ground ginger and the remaining soy sauce and rice wine or sherry. Pour this mixture over the noodles, mix well and fry for another minute. To serve, arrange the noodles in the centre of a warmed dish and place the meat and vegetables around them.

Chop suey

Chicken Chow Mein

1 small green pepper, seeded
1 small red pepper, seeded
40 g/1½ oz butter
1 small onion, chopped
2 sticks celery, chopped
1½ tablespoons flour
300 ml/½ pint hot chicken stock
  (see page 6)
2 tablespoons soy sauce
pepper

150 g/5 oz canned mushrooms,
  drained and sliced
225 g/8 oz cooked chicken
  breast, chopped
225 g/8 oz broad Chinese
  noodles
oil for frying
100 g/4 oz flaked almonds, fried
  in butter and salted

Cut the peppers into thin strips and blanch in boiling water for 5 minutes. Remove and drain. Melt 25 g/1 oz of the butter in a pan, add the onion and celery, and fry lightly for 2 minutes. Sprinkle the flour over, add the stock, bring to the boil and simmer for 10 minutes, until the vegetables are just tender. Season with the soy sauce and pepper. Add the pepper strips, mushrooms and chicken breast. Cover the pan and simmer, gently, for 15 minutes.

Bring a pan of salted water to the boil, add the noodles and simmer for 15 minutes. Drain, rinse with cold water and drain again. Set aside one third of the noodles. Add the remaining butter to the rest and put into a warmed serving dish. Cover and keep warm.

Cut the remaining noodles, which must be very well drained, into pieces. Heat the oil in a frying pan and fry the noodles until golden yellow. Drain on absorbent paper. Pour the chicken sauce over the buttered noodles and sprinkle the fried noodles and salted almonds on top. Alternatively, the chicken sauce, buttered noodles, fried noodles and salted almonds can all be served separately.

Below: chicken chow mein

Chinese Steamed Rolls

15 g/½ oz fresh yeast or 2
  teaspoons dried yeast
2 tablespoons sugar
250 ml/8 fl oz warm water
450 g/1 lb flour
2 tablespoons oil
4 spring onions, chopped
  or ½ onion, chopped

1 clove garlic, crushed
450 g/1 lb Chinese roast belly of
  pork (see page 37), finely
  shredded
2 tablespoons soy sauce
½ tablespoon dry sherry
1½ tablespoons cornflour
3 tablespoons water or stock

To make the dough, cream the fresh yeast with the sugar and a little of the water, then add the remaining water. (If using dried yeast, dissolve the sugar in the water, sprinkle on the yeast and stir well.) Leave to stand in a warm place for about 10 minutes.

Meanwhile sift the flour into a bowl. Make a well in the centre and pour in the yeast mixture. Working from the outside in, knead to a soft dough which leaves the sides of the bowl clean (about 10 minutes). Add a little more flour if necessary. Allow the dough to stand in a warm place, covered with a clean cloth, until it has doubled in size.

Meanwhile make the filling. Heat the oil in a pan. Add the onion and garlic and fry until golden. Add the pork and stir over high heat until thoroughly heated through. Add the soy sauce, sherry and remaining sugar and mix in well. Mix the cornflour to a smooth paste in a cup with the water or stock. Stir into the ingredients in the pan until the sauce is thick and shiny. Remove the pan from the heat and allow to cool.

Turn the dough on to a floured surface. Knead again for 1 to 2 minutes to knock out air bubbles. Shape into a sausage 5 cm/2 inches thick, and cut into slices 2 cm/¾ inch thick. Roll these slices out until they are 7.5–10 cm/3–4 inches across. Divide the filling among the dough slices, heaping it up in the centre. Fold the edges upwards so that the filling is completely enclosed, and shape into a ball. Cut circles of aluminium foil or greaseproof paper just large enough for the rolls to stand on. Place each roll on a circle inside a steamer, over a pan of boiling water. Steam the rolls 2 cm/¾ inch apart, a few at a time, for 15 to 20 minutes, or until the topsides are shiny and firm. These rolls can be eaten either hot or cold.

Chinese steamed rolls

Overleaf: sukiyaki

Sukiyaki *(see pages 68–69)*

200 g/7 oz transparent noodles
15 g/½ oz dried Chinese black fungus
850 g/1¾ lb fillet steak, thinly sliced
40 g/1½ oz suet or pork fat
400 g/14 oz long-grain rice
4 onions
4 leeks
225 g/8 oz white cabbage
450 g/1 lb canned bamboo shoots
225 g/8 oz spinach, washed and picked over
225 g/8 oz fresh bean sprouts, cleaned
or 225 g/8 oz canned bean sprouts, drained
4 egg yolks

SAUCE
300 ml/½ pint shoyu sauce
or 300 ml/½ pint soy sauce
80 ml/3 fl oz sake
2 teaspoons sugar

Put the noodles and black fungus into separate bowls. Pour on boiling water and leave to soak and swell up for 20 minutes, changing the water twice. Arrange the slices of meat on a dish like petals, with the lump of suet or pork fat in the centre. Cover with aluminium foil and place in the refrigerator until required.

Bring a pan of salted water to the boil, add the rice and simmer for 15 minutes, until tender. Meanwhile cut the onions and leeks into rings. Cut out the cabbage stalk, take the leaves apart and wash and drain them. Halve or quarter the larger leaves. Drain the bamboo shoots, reserving their liquid. Cut into thin slices. Drain the noodles and black fungus. Arrange all the raw ingredients, including the meat, round the grill or gas ring on the table in individual bowls or plates.

To make the sauce, bring the shoyu or soy sauce to the boil in a pan with the sake, sugar and 4 tablespoons of the reserved bamboo shoot liquid. Put in a bowl and place on the table. Drain the rice, rinse with boiling water, drain again and place on the table in a bowl.

Sukiyaki is cooked in the following way. Rub round the inside of the cooking pan with the piece of suet or fat. Set it over the heat, add a quarter of the meat and fry quickly, stirring. Push the meat to one side of the pan and pour some of the sauce over it. Add a quarter of all the remaining ingredients (except the rice and egg) and fry gently, stirring, for 3 minutes. The meat and vegetables are then divided between the guests; the cooked vegetables are dipped in the egg yolk before being eaten. While the first portion of meat and vegetables is being eaten the second is being prepared in the same way, and so on until all the ingredients have been cooked. Each guest seasons his food to taste with the sauce and helps himself to rice.

It is a good idea to take turns over the cooking, to avoid having one person always attending to the pan. Green tea is the correct drink to accompany sukiyaki with a cup or bowl of warm sake afterwards.

Jo Chon Bau

Chinese parcels of yeast dough stuffed with meat

600 g/1¼ lb pork escalopes
2 onions
1 leek
50 g/2 oz butter
salt

FIRST MARINADE
4 tablespoons tomato ketchup
1 tablespoon vinegar
1 teaspoon mild paprika
3 drops Tabasco sauce
1 teaspoon curry powder

SECOND MARINADE
90 ml/3½ fl oz soy sauce
1 tablespoon dry sherry
1 tablespoon honey
ground ginger

DOUGH
20 g/¾ oz fresh yeast
or 1 tablespoon dried yeast
1 teaspoon sugar
300 ml/½ pint warm water
400 g/14 oz flour
½ teaspoon salt

Pat the pork escalopes dry with absorbent paper. Trim off any fat.

To make the first marinade, mix together the tomato ketchup, vinegar, paprika, Tabasco sauce and curry powder. Put the meat in a bowl, cover with the marinade, and leave for 10 minutes to absorb the flavours. Meanwhile brush the grill rack with oil and put the grill pan underneath to catch any drips. Remove the escalopes from the marinade, drain and grill for 10 minutes each side. Alternatively fry the meat in a little oil, over gentle heat, for 10 minutes each side.

While the meat is cooking prepare the second marinade: warm the soy sauce and sherry in a saucepan. Add the honey and stir until dissolved. Season with a pinch ground ginger and take the pan off the heat. Remove the pork escalopes from the grill or frying pan, cut into cubes 1 cm/½ inch square, and add to the pan. Cover and leave to stand for 45 minutes.

Jo chon bau

To make the dough, cream the fresh yeast with the sugar and a little of the water, then add the remaining water. (If using dried yeast, dissolve the sugar in the water, sprinkle on the yeast and stir well.) Leave to stand in a warm place for about 10 minutes.

Meanwhile, sift the flour and salt into a bowl. Make a well in the centre and pour in the yeast mixture. Working from the outside in, knead to a soft dough which leaves the sides of the bowl clean (about 10 minutes). Add a little more flour if necessary. Allow the dough to stand in a warm place, covered with a clean cloth, until it doubles in size.

Meanwhile cut the onions into strips. Cut the leek in half lengthways, wash and drain, and cut into pieces 5 mm/¼ inch long. Then heat 25 g/1 oz of the butter in a frying pan, add the onions and leek pieces and fry for 5 minutes, stirring. Remove the pieces of meat from the second marinade, drain and add to the pan. Season with salt and stew all together for 5 minutes.

Turn the dough on to a floured surface. Knead again for 1 to 2 minutes to knock out air bubbles. Then roll out and divide into 8 portions. Form each portion into a circular shape with your hands, put some of the meat mixture into the centre of each circle, and fold the dough into parcels, pressing the edges well together. Melt the remaining butter and paint it over the dough parcels. Cover a roasting grid with foil, grease the foil with margarine, and place the dough parcels on it. Place the grid on a roasting pan partly filled with water. Roast for 20 minutes at 240°C/475°F/gas 9. Remove from the oven and serve.

Siu Mai

Savoury dumplings

SERVES 8–10

3 dried Chinese mushrooms
350 g/12 oz lean pork, chopped
100 g/4 oz fat ham, chopped
1 frozen Pacific prawn, thawed and chopped
1 walnut-sized piece bamboo, chopped
2 water chestnuts (optional), chopped

1 tablespoon sake, Chinese rice wine or dry sherry
1 teaspoon soy sauce
few drops sesame oil
½ teaspoon sugar
1 egg white, beaten
salt, pepper
10 egg or spring roll wrappers

Soak the mushrooms in hot water for 15 to 30 minutes, until swollen. Squeeze them dry, remove the stalks and cut the caps into short, thin strips. Mix together all the ingredients except the egg roll wrappers, and set the mixture aside for 1 hour.

Meanwhile take the egg roll wrappers one at a time, and cut out 4 circles of 10 cm/4 inches diameter from each; use a pastry cutter or saucer of the right diameter. Divide the filling into 40 equal portions and shape into balls. Place each on a circle of dough. Fold the edges upward over the filling and crimp carefully together. Hold the dumpling a little way above a pastry board and let it drop a few times to flatten the underside and settle the filling. There must be no air between the filling and the dough case. Continue in this way until all the dumplings have been shaped, keeping the egg roll wrappers and the completed dumplings covered with polythene sheets as you work.

Steam the dumplings for 20 to 30 minutes. Place a small piece of aluminium foil under each dumpling to prevent sticking to the bottom of the steamer. If you only have a small steamer, the dumplings can be steamed in batches, then all heated up together before serving. Serve as an hors d'oeuvre or lunch dish, with an accompanying dip of chilli sauce.

Siu mai

EGG DISHES

Japanese Egg Salad

200 g/7 oz canned tuna fish,
  drained
200 g/7 oz canned mandarin
  oranges, drained
4 hard-boiled eggs, sliced
50 g/2 oz stuffed green olives,
  sliced

2 tablespoons oil
juice 1 lemon
2 tablespoons soy sauce
salt, pepper
sugar
sprigs parsley

Flake the fish into a bowl. Add the mandarin oranges, eggs
and olives and mix together lightly. To make the dressing,
mix together the oil, lemon juice and soy sauce. Season to
taste with salt, pepper and a pinch sugar. Pour over the salad.
Stand the salad in the refrigerator, covered, for 10 minutes to
absorb the flavours. To serve, divide the salad between four
glass dishes and garnish each with a sprig of parsley.

Japanese egg salad

Chinese Tea Eggs

MAKES 6

2 litres/3½ pints water
2 tablespoons jasmine tea

100 g/4 oz sugar
6 hard-boiled eggs (unshelled)

Bring the water to the boil in a pan. Add the tea and sugar,
and continue to boil for 15 minutes. Strain the liquid, bring
back to the boil and allow to simmer gently for 1 hour. Tap
the egg shells on all sides to crack evenly, but do not peel
them. Put them in the tea and simmer gently for another
hour. Then take the eggs out of the tea and remove the shells.
The egg whites will have an attractive marbled appearance.
Serve either hot or cold.

Crayfish Fu Yung

juice ½ lemon
100 g/4 oz fresh mushrooms,
  sliced
2 egg whites
1 teaspoon strong chicken
  stock
salt, pepper
150 ml/¼ pint oil
325 g/11 oz canned crayfish,
  drained

100 g/4 oz canned bamboo
  shoots, drained and thinly
  sliced
1 teaspoon cornflour
1 tablespoon water
1 teaspoon soy sauce
2 tablespoons Chinese rice wine
  or dry sherry
100 g/4 oz cooked ham, diced

Bring a pan of salted water to the boil. Add the lemon juice
and mushrooms and simmer for 5 minutes, until tender.
Drain and keep warm.

Mix the egg whites and stock together; season with salt
and pepper. Heat the oil in a pan without letting it get too
hot. Add the egg white mixture and let it solidify to a smooth,
soft consistency. Tip into a sieve and reserve the oil. Pour 3
tablespoons oil back into the pan and reheat. Remove any
horny strips from the crayfish and add the crayfish to the pan
with the mushrooms and bamboo shoots. Season with salt
and pepper and fry for 2 minutes. Then mix in the egg white
mixture. Separately, mix the cornflour, water, soy sauce and
rice wine or sherry together. Add to the pan and fry over high
heat for 30 seconds. Transfer to a warmed dish and garnish
with the ham.

Fu yung hay

Fu Yung Hay

2 cloves garlic
salt, pepper, ground ginger
100 ml/4 fl oz oil
350 g/12 oz tomatoes, skinned,
  seeded and chopped
1 teaspoon sugar
2 tablespoons soy sauce
150 g/5 oz frozen petits pois

butter
1 leek, thinly sliced
2 onions, thinly sliced
8 small, tender sticks celery,
  thinly sliced
8 eggs, beaten
300 g/10 oz canned crawfish
  tails, drained

To make the tomato sauce, crush the garlic with salt. Heat 2 tablespoons oil in a pan and fry the garlic for 2 minutes, until pale yellow. Add the tomatoes and stew, stirring, until you have a thick sauce. Season with the sugar, soy sauce and a small pinch ground ginger, and keep warm.

Bring a pan of salted water to the boil, add the peas, cover, and simmer for 5 minutes, until done. Drain the peas, add a knob of butter and keep warm.

To make the omelets, heat 2 tablespoons oil in a pan. Add the leek, onions and celery and fry for 5 minutes, stirring. Then stir the vegetable mixture into the eggs. Remove any horny strips from the crawfish tails, then stir the tails into the eggs. Season to taste. For each omelet, put 1 tablespoon of the remaining oil in a pan. Heat until it is smoking and ladle in a quarter of the egg mixture. Fry over low heat for 5 minutes, shaking the pan from time to time. The omelets should be cooked in quick succession, slid on to warm plates and kept hot. When all the omelets have been cooked, scatter the peas round the edge and serve at once. Hand the tomato sauce separately.

VEGETABLES

Chinese Cabbage

2 Chinese cabbages   grated nutmeg
20g/$\frac{3}{4}$oz butter

Shred the cabbage leaves, cut them into finger-length pieces, or leave them whole, according to taste. Wash and drain. Bring a pan of salted water to the boil, add the cabbage and simmer for 20 to 25 minutes, until tender. (The quicker it is cooked the better.) Drain and return to the pan. Add the butter and shake over gentle heat until the butter has melted and the cabbage is coated. Sprinkle with grated nutmeg and serve.

Braised Chinese Cabbage

2 Chinese cabbages, quartered   300ml/$\frac{1}{2}$ pint stock
salt   1–2 tablespoons soy sauce
50g/2oz streaky bacon, chopped   1 tablespoon chopped parsley
1 onion, chopped

Season the cabbages lightly with salt. Melt the bacon in a pan until the fat runs. Add the onion and brown slightly. Add the cabbage and fry quickly, but do not allow to brown. Pour the stock into the pan and simmer for 20 minutes, until the cabbage is tender. Season with soy sauce and more salt if necessary. Transfer to a warmed bowl and serve garnished with parsley.

Braised Chinese cabbage

Chinese Cabbage, Stir-fried

1 dried Chinese mushroom
2 Chinese cabbages
2 tablespoons oil
½ tablespoon salt
1 small piece root ginger, finely
  chopped
100 ml/4 fl oz chicken stock (see
  page 6)
¼ teaspoon sugar
1 tablespoon soy sauce
2 teaspoons cornflour
1 tablespoon water

Soak the mushroom in hot water for 15 to 30 minutes, until swollen. Drain well, remove the stalk and cut the cap into long, thin strips. Cut off the thick stalk from the cabbage. Wash the leaves and shred them into fairly short pieces.

Heat the oil in a wok or other lidded, heavy pan. Add the salt and ginger, and turn in the oil over high heat for 30 seconds. Add the cabbage and mushroom and fry, turning over continuously, for 1½ minutes. Add the stock, sugar and soy sauce, reduce the heat slightly, place the lid on the pan, and let the ingredients simmer gently for 2 minutes. Meanwhile mix the cornflour to a smooth paste with the water. Then stir this solution into the pan until the sauce thickens and becomes shiny. Serve as an accompaniment to Chinese roast belly of pork (see page 37), or other meat dishes.

Chinese Mixed Vegetables

10 g/⅓ oz dried Chinese black
  fungus
100 g/4 oz white cabbage
100 g/4 oz carrots, peeled
100 g/4 oz cucumber, peeled
100 g/4 oz canned bamboo
  shoots, drained
4 tablespoons sesame seed oil
50 g/2 oz frozen peas
150 ml/¼ pint hot chicken stock
  (see page 6)
2 tablespoons soy sauce
salt
sugar

Soak the fungus in warm water for 15 to 30 minutes, until swollen. Meanwhile cut the cabbage, carrots, cucumber and bamboo shoots into conveniently-sized strips. Drain the fungus and cut into pieces. Heat the oil in a frying pan and fry the cabbage, stirring, for 2 minutes. Stir in the fungus, carrots, cucumber, bamboo shoots and peas and heat through. Add the stock. Season with the soy sauce and a pinch of salt and sugar. Simmer over low heat for 15 minutes, stirring occasionally. Serve at once.

Chinese mixed vegetables

Bebotok

Cabbage rolls

400 g/14 oz minced beef
2 tablespoons finely chopped
  onion
1 clove garlic, crushed
1 chilli pepper, shredded
  or ½ teaspoon chilli sauce
1½ tablespoons ground coriander
½ tablespoon ground cumin
6 blanched almonds, chopped
½ teaspoon galingale (optional)

½ teaspoon soft brown sugar
3 tablespoons grated coconut
  (preferably fresh)
½ teaspoon belacan (prawn
  paste)
1 teaspoon salt
1 egg, lightly beaten
8–10 large, white or green
  cabbage leaves

Put all the ingredients except the cabbage leaves into a large bowl, and work together until the mixture becomes tacky and sticks together. Add a little milk if the mixture is too dry. Divide the mixture into 8 to 10 equal portions, forming each into a slightly flattened ball. Bring a pan of water to the boil, add the cabbage leaves, and simmer until they are soft enough to be folded without breaking. Rinse and drain well. Lay one portion of the filling on each of the leaves, fold the leaves up into a package and secure with cocktail sticks.

Place the rolls in a steamer over a pan of boiling water. Steam the rolls for 20 to 25 minutes with the lid on, until cooked. Remove from the steamer and serve.

Chinese Stuffed Mushrooms

8 dried Chinese mushrooms
100–175 g/4–6 oz lean pork,
  shredded
1 tablespoon chopped onion
1 small piece root ginger, finely
  chopped

1 tablespoon finely chopped
  bamboo shoots
  or 1 tablespoon finely
  chopped water chestnuts
½ tablespoon soy sauce
½ tablespoon dry sherry
½ teaspoon oil
1 tablespoon chopped parsley

Make sure the mushrooms are large and unbroken. Soak the mushrooms in hot water for 15 to 30 minutes, until swollen. Drain well and remove the stalks. Mix together the pork, onion, ginger, bamboo shoots or water chestnuts, soy sauce, sherry and oil. Fill the mushroom caps with this mixture, pressing down firmly. Place them close together on a flat dish or dinner plate, cover loosely with a sheet of aluminium foil, and steam for 30 minutes, with the lid on. Transfer to a warm dish, sprinkle with the parsley and serve as an hors d'oeuvre to a Chinese meal.

Note: If you cannot get dried Chinese mushrooms, use large, flat, fresh mushrooms.

Chinese Mushrooms

Tung-ku-nidng-jou

25 g/1 oz dried Chinese black
  fungus
3 tablespoons soy sauce
1 tablespoon Chinese rice wine
  or dry sherry
1 teaspoon sugar
1 tablespoon cornflour

225 g/8 oz lean minced pork
4 canned water chestnuts,
  drained and chopped
salt
2 tablespoons oil
sprigs parsley

Soak the fungus in warm water for 15 to 30 minutes, until swollen. Drain in a sieve, reserving the water. Cut off and discard any stalks. To make the stuffing, mix together in a bowl 1 tablespoon of the soy sauce, the rice wine or sherry, sugar and cornflour. Stir in the pork and water chestnuts, and season with salt.

Heat the oil in a large frying pan. Place the fungus in the pan, rounded side downwards. Divide the stuffing between the fungus and spread it flat with a knife. Fry the fungus over moderate heat for 1 minute, until the undersides are slightly browned. Pour 4 tablespoons of the reserved soaking water into the pan, bring to the boil, cover the pan, and stew for 15 minutes over very low heat.

Remove the fungus carefully from the pan with a slotted spoon, and arrange on a warmed dish, stuffing side up. Add the remaining soy sauce to the pan and reheat the liquid, stirring. Pour the sauce over the fungus, garnish with the parsley and serve.

Note: If you cannot get dried Chinese black fungus, use large, flat, fresh mushrooms.

Right: Chinese mushrooms

Bamboo Shoot Salad

1 clove garlic
salt, ground ginger
2 tablespoons soy sauce
3 tablespoons vinegar
2 tablespoons oil
2 hard-boiled eggs, chopped
1 red pepper, seeded and
 chopped
sugar
250 g/9 oz canned bamboo
 shoots, drained and sliced
½ sweet pickled cucumber
¼ cooked celeriac root
1 tablespoon chopped tarragon
1 tablespoon chopped dill

Crush the garlic with salt. Stir together a pinch of ground ginger, the soy sauce, vinegar and oil to make a smooth dressing. Mix together the eggs and pepper and season with salt and sugar. Then mix with the dressing and stand in the refrigerator for 20 minutes. Mix together the bamboo shoots, cucumber and celeriac. Pour the chilled dressing over the vegetables and mix carefully. Garnish with the chopped herbs and serve.

Chinese Spring Onion Tassels

spring onions, as required

These decorations are always made from spring onions, even though they are sometimes referred to as shallot tassels. In Chinese cooking they are used as an edible garnish with many dishes.

Trim off the root as closely as possible. Cut away all except 7·5 cm/3 inches of the green stem. With a very sharp knife, cut down the green stem to a depth of 2–2·5 cm/¾–1 inch, and then make a second cut at right angles to it. Bend the four strips out slightly. Place the onions in a bowl of iced water, containing a few ice cubes, until the ends curl over. The same effect can be obtained by moistening the onions, and then putting them in the frozen-food compartment of a refrigerator, again just until the ends curl over.

Bamboo shoot salad

DESSERTS

Lychees

Lychees, popular as they are in Europe, originally come from China. The fruits are almost round, have a scaly red skin, and grow in clusters on trees about 9 m/30 feet high. They have been popular in China since ancient times. Their flesh is firm and white and their flavour is slightly reminiscent of cherries, with a touch of nutmeg. Nowadays canned lychees are available in oriental food shops and are on the menu of every Chinese restaurant.

Today lychees are also grown in South Africa, India, Australia, Hawaii, Brazil and Florida. Fresh lychees are imported to Europe from South Africa, the season being December to April, and from Pakistan and India in May and June. Hong Kong is the main source of canned lychees. These are preserved in syrup. The Chinese almost always eat the fruit cooked, or dried; hence another name for the lychee is Chinese hazelnut. Lychees are also a rich source of Vitamin C.

Chinese Honey Apples

2 eggs	4 dessert apples, peeled
100 g/4 oz flour	4 tablespoons oil
150 ml/¼ pint water	100 g/4 oz honey
salt	4 tablespoons groundnut oil

To make the batter, mix together the eggs, flour, water and a pinch salt in a bowl. Remove the apple cores with an apple corer; cut the apples into thick rounds. Heat the first quantity of oil in a frying pan. Dip the apple rings into the batter, then fry them in the hot oil for 3 minutes each side, until golden brown. Heat the honey and groundnut oil in a pan. Dip the fried apple rings in this mixture and allow to cool.

Note: In China a bowl of water with ice cubes in it is served with this dessert. The freshly-fried apple rings are speared on chopsticks and dipped into the water so that the honey crystallises.

Peking Dust

450 g/1 lb unsweetened, canned	1 tablespoon soft dark
chestnut purée	brown sugar
150 ml/¼ pint water	100 g/4 oz granulated sugar
500 ml/18 fl oz whipping cream	mandarin orange segments,
3 tablespoons castor sugar	blanched almonds, walnuts
1 teaspoon vanilla sugar	and glacé cherries to decorate

Mix together in a bowl the chestnut purée and 80 ml/3 fl oz of the water. Put the cream in another bowl and beat until it begins to thicken. Add the castor sugar and vanilla sugar and beat the cream until stiff. Remove half of the cream from the bowl and blend it into the chestnut purée mixture with the brown sugar. Bring the remaining water and the white sugar to the boil in a pan. Boil, stirring constantly, until a thick syrup is formed.

Dip the fruits and nuts (use as many as or as few as you wish) into this syrup, and then leave them to cool and harden on a piece of waxed paper. Put the chestnut purée mixture in an icing bag. Using a nozzle with a small round opening, (i.e. not toothed), squeeze the mixture out in small lengths and heap them up on a dish. Cover with the remaining whipped cream and decorate with the glazed fruits and nuts.

Lychees

78

Korean caramelised bananas

Korean Caramelised Bananas

4 bananas, peeled
20 g/¾ oz cornflour
2 egg whites, beaten
flour for coating
oil for deep frying

15 g/½ oz butter
100 g/4 oz sugar
2 tablespoons water
25 g/1 oz sesame seeds

Cut the bananas into pieces 2 cm/¾ inch long. Mix the cornflour into the egg whites. Sprinkle some flour on a plate. Dip the banana pieces first in the flour, then in the egg white mixture, and deep fry them until golden brown. Remove and drain on absorbent paper.

To make the sauce, gently heat the butter and sugar in a pan until golden brown. Stir in the water and sesame seeds. Add the fried banana pieces and turn carefully in the sauce. Transfer to a warmed and greased dish and serve.

Peking Pears

4 ripe pears, peeled
4 tablespoons honey
50 g/2 oz chopped walnuts

1 teaspoon lemon juice
ground ginger

Remove the cores from the pears with an apple corer. Mix together in a bowl the honey, walnuts, lemon juice and a small pinch ginger. Put this stuffing inside the pears. Grease an ovenproof dish and set the pears upright in it. Cover the dish, place on the bottom shelf of the oven and bake for 40 minutes at 200°C/400°F/gas 6. Remove the lid from the dish 10 minutes before the end of the cooking time. Serve at once.

INDEX